Corner tower at Roscommon Castle

THE CASTLES
OF CONNACHT

Mike Salter

FOLLY PUBLICATIONS

ACKNOWLEDGEMENTS

The illustrations in this book are mostly the product of the author's own site surveys since 1971. Plans redrawn from his field note books are mostly reproduced to scales of 1:400 for keeps, tower houses, stronghouses and the like, and 1:800 for courtyard castles and bawns, whilst large bawns are shown at 1:2000. The author would like to acknowledge with thanks assistance from the following individuals. Max Barfield drove on the 1992 trip and provided the photo of Ballymote and also that of Parke's Castle on the back cover. John Lowe provided photos of Castle Hacket and Furmina. Maureen Costello of Castlebar Library provided information on several Mayo castles. Helen Thomas drove the author through all five counties of Connacht during the summer of 2003 and checked through the text. Eamon Cody and several other members of staff at the National Monuments Section of the Department of the Environment, Heritage and Local Government in Dublin provided much advice and information. About ten of the plans are at least partly based on notes or drawings in their archaeological records. Thanks also to the staff of the map section at the Bodleian Library in Oxford, to Peter Hays for several useful comments, and to Ken McLeod for a considerable amount of advice and help and the use of his maps.

AUTHOR'S NOTES

This book is one of a series of five volumes superseding the author's previous work Castles and Stronghouses of Ireland, published in 1993 and now out of print. It is part of a series of books about castles in Britain and Ireland all in a similar style with plans on a set of common metric scales allowing useful comparisons of sizes, wall thicknesses, etc. It is recommended that visitors use the Ordnance Survey 1:50,000 maps to locate the monuments, and grid references are given in the gazetteers. The book is intended as a portable field guide giving as much information and illustrative material as possible in a book of modest size, weight and price, especially providing material about buildings not properly described elsewhere in print. The aim has been to give some basic information about owners or custodians of castles but no attempt has been made to provide detailed family genealogical histories. Ghost stories, myths and legends are not normally included, and personalities later than the 1690s are generally only mentioned if of importance to an understanding of a building's development.

All dimensions are given in metres and usually refer to the size of the building at or near ground level, but above the plinth if there is one. Most towers and hall-houses will be smaller than the quoted dimensions higher up because of the external batter of the walls. The majority of the measurements quoted were personally taken on site by the author. On plans the original work is shown black, post-1800 work is stippled and alterations and additions of intermediate periods are shown hatched. Each level is called a storey, sleeping and storage lofts tucked under vaults being treated as full storeys, and the basement being the first or lowest storey with its floor at or near ground level unless mentioned as otherwise. An attic room entirely within the height of a gabled roof is usually mentioned as an extra level additional to the number of storeys given.

ABOUT THE AUTHOR

Mike Salter is 50 and has been a professional writer and publisher since 1988. He is particularly interested in the planning and layout of medieval buildings and has a huge collection of plans of castles and churches he has measured during tours (mostly by bicycle and motorcycle) throughout all parts of the British Isles since 1968. Wolverhampton born and bred, Mike now lives in an old cottage beside the Malvern Hills. His other interests include walking, maps, railways, board games, morris dancing and playing percussion instruments and calling folk dances with an occasional folk group.

First published January 2004. Copyright 2004 Mike Salter.
Folly Publications, Folly Cottage, 151 West Malvern Rd, Malvern Worcs WR14 4AY
Printed by Aspect Design, 89 Newtown Rd, Malvern, Worcs WR14 2PD.

Ardtermon Castle

CONTENTS

A map of extant castles appears inside the front cover

Old print of Moygara Castle

INTRODUCTION

The word castle means a fortified place serving as a residence, administrative centre and status symbol of a feudal lord. As such castles were essentially an import to Ireland with the Anglo-Norman invasion of the 1160s and 70s, since the word was rarely used in Ireland beforehand. The Irish chiefs built crannogs or artificial islands in lakes and forts with dry-stone ramparts (some of which remained in use as late as the 17th century) but these were not castles. Although the first castles built by the Norman invaders were of earth and wood rather than stone, they took a more tower-like form than the previous forts, thus emphasising the pre-eminence of the lord, and they had a much greater importance as administrative and judicial centres than anything built beforehand in Ireland. In these new castles a timber tower or house surrounded by a small palisaded court as a dwelling for the lord was raised up on a high earth mound or motte whilst an accompanying court or bailey at a lower level contained a hall, chapel, and all the stores, workshops and other farm buildings required by the lord's household within a rampart and palisade with a ditch outside. Mottes are essentially artificial mounds, although natural hillocks and spurs (and in some cases older raths) were often reshaped to create them. The early years of the Anglo-Norman invasion of Ireland had little impact on Connacht and consequently it has the lowest density of motte and bailey castles amongst the four provinces. Early earthworks are noted here and there beside or below later stone castles in the gazetteers, and it is known that some of the seats of Richard de Burgh's followers in Galway (see below) took the form of timber buildings on platforms surrounded by water-filled moats, but essentially this book is concerned with buildings of mortared stone.

In 1227 Henry III gave Richard de Burgh leave to occupy Connacht, then ruled by the O'Connors. He finally took it over in 1235 after being supported by a huge army led by the Justiciar, the O'Connors being left with most of Roscommon, whilst the limestone plains of Galway and Mayo were settled by de Burgh's knights, particularly the de Birminghams, the de Cogans, the FitzGeralds, the de Stauntons and the de Exeters. They immediately began building castles, the most important of which each had a stone building containing the lord's apartments over dark cellars. In this book the term hall house is used for mean a structure of this type originally standing alone without outer defences of stone, whilst the term hall keep is used to refer to buildings like that at Athenry with a surrounding stone curtain wall of about the same period. Both vary quite considerably in size, some being only large enough to contain a single lordly apartment, whilst others appear to have contained two upper rooms end to end, one (usually with a latrine in some sort of projection) clearly more private and secure than the other. Recent fieldwork has revealed more of these buildings than previously known, with a possible total of nearly thirty of them in Connacht. The greatest of them is Castlekirke, a more ambitious building with projecting corner turrets and a porch on one side perched on a rock in Lough Corrib, probably of native Irish origin although in the Anglo-Norman style of building.

Hall-house at Annaghkeen, Co Galway

Doocastle, Co Mayo: traces of vault

Motte at Tulsk, Co Roscommon

The comparatively thinly-walled baileys accompanying the 13th century keeps at Ardrahan, Athenry, Ballylahan, Caherakilleen, Dunmoe, Kiltartan, Rinndown and Templehouse are all now very fragmentary and only footings remain of the keep itself at Ballylahan. This building and Kiltartan (which has by far the largest court) have remains of gatehouses with passageways flanked by U-shaped towers. Athenry lacks a gatehouse but does have two circular towers set at either end of a hall block. Rinndown also has a hall block (an addition of the 1290s) separate from the chamber in the keep, and between the two lies a modest square gatehouse, whilst Templehouse also has a square gatehouse. The gateways at Rinndown and Kiltartan were each furnished with grooves for a portcullis, never a common feature in the castles of Connacht, since they rarely occur in later medieval tower houses and there are no examples in the later bawns. There were, however, portcullises in the huge twin-U-shaped gatehouse of the royal castle built at Roscommon in the 1270s. This building had no separate keep (the gatehouse functioned as such, as in contemporary royal castles in North Wales) and the bailey is more regularly planned and more massively walled that the other examples, with large U-shaped towers at the four corners. In the 1290s the de Burghs erected a similar building at Ballymote, where the corner towers are fully circular, although there are also intermediate towers, two of which are D-shaped. A third, much larger, but less massively built castle of this type dating from c1300 is Ballintober, where the corner towers are polygonal towards the field. All these buildings are low-lying and had water filled moats around them.

After the murder of William de Burgh, Earl of Ulster and Lord of Connacht in 1333 the Gaelic-speaking native Irish began to recover lands at the expense of the Anglo-Normans. In Connacht cadet branches of the de Burgh family took over but became themselves increasingly Gaelic in speech and culture, even their name being Gaelicised as Burke. Thus the Upper MacWilliam Burkes became predominant in Galway and various branches of the Lower MacWilliam Burkes ruled much of Mayo, whilst the O'Connors ruled Roscommon and parts of Sligo, the rest of which by the 16th century was shared between the O'Dowds, the O'Haras, and gallowglas clans such as the MacDonaghs and MacSwineys.

Hall at Athenry, Co Galway

Entrance arch, Garbally, Co Galway

Tower house at Cloonboo, Co Galway   *Moycola Castle, Co Galway*

The vast majority of the castles in Connacht take a form known to modern writers as a tower house although contemporaries simply referred to them as castles. Tower houses are common throughout Ireland, Scotland and the northern parts of England and in the 14th, 15th and 16th centuries were generally regarded as a suitable form of residence for both lords and their most important tenants. The towers were able to withstand attacks of short duration by violent neighbours or bands of raiders and also formed impresive status symbols. Most of the tower houses in Connacht are plain rectangles in plan without any projecting wings or turrets. They seem to have evolved from the hall-houses, several of which were remodelled later on and provided with vaults upon inserted crosswalls and extra upper rooms within former roof spaces. Irish tower houses generally have single undivided basement rooms and either have a graceful batter throughout their height or are battered steeply throughout the height of the lowest level and then rise vertically. Many of the towers have one thick end wall hollowed out to provide a tier of small private chambers, the lowest of which always has a murder hole slot commanding the entrance lobby below. Usually a spiral stair opens off the lobby but sometimes there is a flight of straight steps between the two. Portcullises were rare in tower house entrances. More normal was a combination of an inward opening wooden door and an iron grille or yett opening outwards, the latter being secured with a chain running through a hole in the doorway jamb. There are a number of instances where the end wall containing the staircase and chambers over the entrance was built before the rest of the tower and there are several examples where the intended main body was never added.

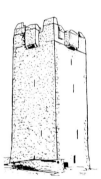

*Carrickkildavnet
Co Mayo*

Castle Kirke

The towers usually have a vault over at least one of the main rooms, commonly the second the storey. The vaults often show signs of the wickerwork mats upon which they were constructed, the mats being left in place after the timber supporting frame was removed. To lighten the load on the outer walls the haunches at each side of a vault were sometimes left hollow, the space often being used to contain what are often known as secret chambers, since the only access to them was usually only by means of a concealed trapdoor from above. In the Gaelic parts of Ireland the topmost room, which was the largest as a result of the walls being much thinner above the vault, was commonly the main hall, with the lord's private room below it. This is the reverse of the usual layout in the English-speaking parts of Ireland, and in tower houses in England and Scotland. It perhaps reflects the differing nature of Gaelic and English society, Gaelic lords being more integrated with their kinsmen and less worried about enjoying the greater personal security and emphasis on status that might result from having their rooms higher up in the building.

The middle storeys of the towers usually have latrines, known in the medieval period as garderobes from the practice of hanging clothes up in the latrine chambers to absorb the urine vapours as a means of controlling parasites. The latrines are often reached by a passage from a window embrasure in a room but Rockfleet has a small latrine chamber opening directly off the stair so that everybody had direct access to it, whilst Lydacan and a few other towers with subsidiary rooms in an end wall have a more sophisticated arrangement in which a latrine placed on the far side of the tower from the spiral stair is reached from it by a passage between the main and subsidiary rooms, the main room below having an arch over one end of it to carry the passage.

Irish tower houses are difficult to date with precision since both plan forms and architectural details, once established, remained in fashion for over two hundred years. A few later towers contain date stones and there are records of the construction of some towers, although many documents were lost during the wars and estate confiscations of the 17th century. Whilst the majority of the towers probably date between the 1470s and the 1540s, buildings such as Roslee lacking in cut stone and having straight staircases throughout all levels could be as early as the 14th century. Fireplaces only seem to have begun to replace central braziers c1500, gunloops suitable for pistols or muskets probably began to appear c1550, and by the late 16th century the upper rooms were sometimes given large mullion-and-transomed windows with hoodmoulds and leaded glass rather than narrow ogival-headed lights closed with internal wooden shutters. The fireplaces of these later towers are often surmounted by high ornamental chimney-stacks, those on side walls sometimes partly or wholly blocking the wall-walk. However, fireplaces and gunloops were sometimes inserted into older towers and hall houses. Brackets are often provided on either side of fireplaces to resist the sideways thrust of their joggled arches of several stones. Gunloops in Irish towers tend to be roughly made circular or square openings, making them inconspicuous from the outside. Features commonly found on Irish towers but unknown outside Ireland are battlements with stepped merlons and the use of loops piercing the corners, usually at third storey level in four storey buildings. A small group of towers built between 1600 and the wars of the 1640s lack vaults over the main rooms, which are each of lesser height. Derryhivenny has five storeys in a tower no taller than earlier structures with just three lofty main levels. A small vaultless tower with tiny corner fireplaces at Castle ffrench is thought to be as late as the 1680s.

Many of the towers have bartizans on at least some of the corners at the top, two set diagonally opposite being the minimum required to cover all four walls with their machicolations. In Connacht these bartizans are nearly always square and are carried on corbels of inverted pyramidal shape. They seem to have been introduced before the use of firearms became common in the early 16th century and remained in fashion until the mid 17th century. Closed-in bartizans containing small corner rooms half-way up a tower also occur occasionally, notably at Aughnanure and on the tower on Clare Island. Projections known as box-machicolations sometimes project from the middle of the sides of a tower, one being very often placed over the entrance doorway. Roofs could be covered with slates or flat stone slabs, although thatch was also sometimes used.

Most of the tower houses now stand alone but about two dozen still have a small walled court called a bawn and originally there must have been many more. Most of the bawns are rectangular and have square or circular corner turrets or bastions known as flankers. These nearly always have gunloops, which suggests that they were mostly added in the second half of the 16th century. At Ballyhowly in Mayo the outer parts of the circular flankers are brought out to a pointed prow to avoid a dead area which could not be covered by gunloops from the adjoining flanker, whilst a bawn closely surrounding the tower at Derrydonnell in Galway has triangular flankers for a similar reason. Bawn walls were often quite thin and those without a wall-walk could only be defended by gunloops at ground level and from the flankers. McPhilbin's in Mayo has a bawn wall just 0.7m thick, yet it still carried a wall-walk formed of wide overhanging slabs, and there was a machicolation over the bawn gateway. Aughnanure is exceptional in preserving almost all of an outer bawn and also parts of an inner bawn and a banqueting hall. Other unusually complete bawns in County Galway are at Dungory, Dunsandle, Fiddaun and Pallas.

In the medieval period castle walls were often whitewashed both inside and out, thus making the best of the limited light admitted through the narrow windows. The lowest rooms were generally used for storage but the living rooms above often had built-in seats in the window embrasures. These rooms might sometimes have wall paintings of biblical, allegorical or heroic scenes, or tapestries or other hangings with similar motifs. Carpets were only introduced in the late 16th century, before which those floors not formed of planks laid on massive beams were made of rammed earth or clay, and all the floors were covered with rushes changed occasionally as thought necessary. Cooking was done on the main fire or in an outbuilding since only a few Irish tower houses (usually those built after 1600) contained kitchens specifically designed as such. The English and Spanish lords found Irish cuisine primitive compared with what they were used to in their home countries. The sort of privacy we now all take for granted did not exist in a medieval castle. Even lords and ladies often had attendants sleeping in the same room or in a passage outside although the lordly bed would usually be curtained or screened off. Furniture was sparse and of the simplest kind. Only the lord and his family were likely to have individual chairs in their room or in the hall, but the hall would contain tables and benches. Also suitable for seating were the chests within which clothes, plate, and other valuables were generally kept. A notable feature of Irish tower houses is the number of lockers within the walls, nearly every window embrasure having one in some towers.

Remains of bawn at Doonfore, Co Sligo

Castletown Castle, Co Sligo

Tower at Derrymaclaughna, Co Galway

Interior of hall-house at Ballycurrin, Co Mayo

During the 16th century the English crown began to make encroachments upon the lands of the Gaelic lords of Connacht. Some eventually submitted and were given English titles, the chief of the Upper MacWilliam Burkes for instance becoming the Earl of Clanricarde. Roscommon Castle was remodelled in the 1580s to provide a secure but comfortable seat for the governors of Connacht appointed periodically by Queen Elizabeth. In Leitrim, Roscommon and Sligo a number of stronghouses, or Jacobean houses equipped with gunloops and machicolations, were erected in the early 17th century by English and Scottish families settled upon lands confiscated from Gaelic chiefs. That at Dromahair has two wings, and that at Manorhamilton goes one better in additionally having four corner flankers and a bawn also with flankers. At Inishcrone the corner flankers are circular, as in the earlier and more tower-like castle of Ballinafad built in the 1590s. Ardtermon and Tully also had circular flankers, and those at Coote Hall have outer prows like those at Ballyhowly. Castle Baldwin is L-planned whilst Ballincar is T-planned and Dundonnell is a plain rectangle set in a rath used as a bawn. The pro-English Earl of Clanricarde and his kinsmen also built houses of this type, a double pile with central corridors and four corner flankers at Portumna, and a house with two projecting wings and bartizans at Glinsk, whilst another branch of this family built an H-shaped building at Dunamon. The O'Dowds built a plain rectangle with two corner bartizans at Cottlestown. There are also fairly complete (if rather altered) ranges of this period added to older towers at Deel and Rappa in Mayo. Although the thickness of the walls at these houses varies none of them have any vaults, nor are there chambers, latrines or staircases inside the thickness of their walls, all the stairs and internal dividing walls being of wood and having perished long ago.

Monivea Castle, Co Galway

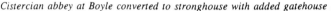

Cistercian abbey at Boyle converted to stronghouse with added gatehouse

Former stronghouse at Tully, Co Roscommon

Ardnabrone Castle, Co Sligo

Many castles in Connacht were damaged during the wars of the 1641-53 and 1689-91 and most of those which survived were abandoned during the 18th century as the gentry moved out into more comfortable new houses or simply moved elsewhere. A lot of the remaining towers in Mayo have lost one wall, probably the result of Cromwellian slighting. Deel and Rockfleet are the only Mayo tower houses still with original wall-walks with parapets, and Rosslee is the only one in Sligo, although there are a number of fairly complete towers in Galway, and several of the 17th century stronghouses are in a fairly complete condition. However, of over 330 castles still remaining in whole or in part in Connacht less than one tenth of them have any part of their structure covered with any sort of roof. Most of these buildings have been renovated from a state of total ruin over the last thirty years, restoration work still being ongoing at several towers, and none of them retain original medieval floors, roofs, doors or window shutters.

FURTHER READING

Castles In Ireland, Tom McNeill, 1997
The Architecture of Ireland, Maurice Craig, 1982
The Medieval Castles of Ireland, David Sweetman, 1999
Irish Castles and Castellated Houses, Harold Leask, 1941
Guide to the National Monuments of Ireland, Peter Harbison, 1970
The Shell Guide to Ireland, Lord Killanin and Michael Duignan, 1969
Archaeological inventories by OPW exist for West Galway, 1993, & North Galway, 1999.
See also the annual proceedings of the Royal Irish Academy, Journal of the Royal Society
    of Antiquaries of Ireland, Galway Archeological Society, and Medieval Archaeology.
Guide pamphlets exist for: Athenry, Aughnanure, Parke's, and Portumna

ACCESS TO THE CASTLES

The following codes appear after the O.S. grid references in the gazetteers. They give only an indication since access arrangements may change from time to time, as may the amount of vegetation obscuring distant views, whilst some monuments may only be open during the summer months. Sites not given a code lie on private land and can only be seen by obtaining prior permission from the landowners. Only occasionally will a courteous request for access by those with a genuine interest in ancient buildings be refused outright, although some owners may forbid visitors to enter ruins considered precarious. Visitors should in all cases close any gates that they need to open, ensure that their dogs do not cause any kind of nuisance to the farmers or their animals, and generally follow the maxim of taking away only photographs and leaving behind nothing but footprints.

A - Free access on foot to the whole site at any time. Mostly sites in state care.
B - Free access on foot to the exterior only at any time. Mostly sites in state care.
C - Private, but clearly visible from public road, path, graveyard, or other open space.
D - Private, but distant view usually possible from road, path or other open space.
E - Open to the public (fee usually payable) during certain hours (at least in summer).
G - Private, but fairly easy courtesy access is currently normally possible.
H - Buildings in use as hotels, shops, museums, etc. Exterior access usually possible.

A GLOSSARY OF TERMS

BAILEY - Defensible space enclosed by a wall or palisade and ditch. BARTIZAN - A turret corbelled out from a corner. BAWN - An enclosure, usually modest in size, surrounded by a wall. CORBEL - A projecting bracket supporting other stonework or timber beams. HALL-HOUSE - A two storey building containing a hall or chamber over a basement. HOODMOULD - Projecting moulding above an arch or lintel to throw off water. JAMB - A side of a doorway, window or other opening. KEEP - A citadel or ultimate strongpoint. The term is not medieval and such buildings were then called donjons. LIGHT - A compartment of a window. LINTEL - Beam spanning an opening. Fireplace lintels are sometimes made of several stones with joggled (zig-zag) joints to prevent slipping. LOOP - A small opening for light or for the discharge of missiles. MACHICOLATION - A slot for dropping stones or shooting missiles at assailants. MERLONS - The upstanding parts of an embattled or crenellated parapet, the cutaway parts being crenels. MOAT - A ditch, water filled or dry, around an enclosure. MULLION - A vertical member dividing the lights of a window. MURDER-HOLE - An internal machicolation, often in the vault of an entrance lobby. OGIVAL-ARCH - Arch of oriental origin with both convex and concave curves. OILLET - Small round opening. PARAPET - A wall for protection at any sudden drop. PLINTH - The projecting base of a wall. PORTCULLIS - Gate designed to rise and fall in vertical grooves, being hoisted up by a windlass. SOFFIT - The underside of an arch. SPANDREL - A surface between an arch and the rectangle containing it. STRONGHOUSE - A mansion capable of defence against attack. TOWER HOUSE - Self contained defensible house with the main rooms stacked vertically. TRACERY - Intersecting ribwork in head of window. TRANSOM - A horizontal member dividing the lights of a window. VOUSSOIR - Small wedge-shaped stone used to form an arch. WALL-WALK - A walkway upon a wall.

GAZETTEER OF CASTLES IN COUNTY GALWAY

AILLE M655123 G

In 1574 MacWilliam Roe held this tower, which measures 13m by 10m and is 13m high to the wall-walk, where there are square bartizans on the NW and SW corners and a circular bartizan on the SE corner. The east wall contains two levels of chambers over the entrance passage with a portcullis groove, the upper chamber being level with the second storey vault. There are spiral stairs in the NE corner to begin with but the third storey is reached by straight stairs going west in the north wall and a second flight returning east again. The first and second storeys have latrines in the SE corner and the second and third storeys both have fireplaces. The third storey has small chambers in the western corners.

ANBALLY M410412 D

This tower measuring 12m by 12.4m was held by a Captain Burke in 1641. It lies in the NW corner of a bawn 31m by 35m, the 1.4m thick wall of which is best preserved on the west, where it contains a latrine near the south end. An earth and stone bank encloses an outer bawn about 100m square to the north, east and south. The entrance in the tower south wall is recessed to allow an outer murder-hole in addition to a wider inner one from a large mural chamber above. The inner doorway into the cellar has a drawbar slot and a passage leads to a spiral stair in the SE corner. The second and third storeys both have latrines in the NE corner. The second storey is vaulted and has a fireplace awkwardly located beside a window embrasure in the NW corner. Another fireplace on the west side has probably been created later out of a window embrasure, and the gables at the summit, providing for an attic without a wall-walk, must also represent a later remodelling.

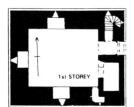

1st STOREY   2nd STOREY   3rd STOREY

0   5
metres

Plans of Aille Castle

Anbally Castle

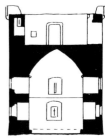

Aille: Section

0   3
m

1st STOREY

Annaghdown: plan

ANNAGHDOWN   M288377 D

The five storey tower by the east shore of Lough Corrib is said to have been built by the last of the bishops of Annaghdown (appointed 1421) before the archbishop of Tuam had the bishopric suppressed. It was held by Nicholas Lynch in 1574 and is now being restored. It measures 11.2m by 10.1m over walls up to 2.6m thick and has a vault over the third storey, a fourth storey with two fireplaces, suggesting a division into two bedchambers, and a fifth storey within the roof gables which are surmounted by chimneystacks. The SE wall contains the entrance with a long narrow chamber south of it and access to a straight stair in the NE wall, leading to where a spiral stair rises in the north corner. The north and east corners retain corbels for bartizans and there was once another on the south corner.

Aille Castle

ANNAGHKEEN   M205447 C

A latrine turret 4m wide projects 3m from the west end of the 16m long NW side of this 13th century hall-house by the east shore of Lough Corrib which in 1574 was held by Moyler MacReamon (Burke). The building is 10.4m wide over side walls 1.6m thick and has upper and lower mural stairs in the NE wall and upper and lower doorways (the later with a drawbar-slot) at the east end of the 15.3m long SE wall. The upper chamber has one narrow loop plus two window embrasures for former two-light windows, one of which has a stair up to a third storey room in the turret and to another upper room later created at this end of the main building. A wall fragment to the SW was part of a later outbuilding or bawn wall. See page 4.

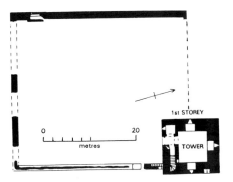

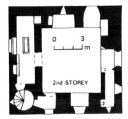

Plans of Anbally Castle

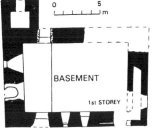

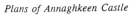

Plans of Annaghkeen Castle

Doorway arch at Aille

Ardfry Castle

Ardamullivan Castle

Plan of Ardfry Castle (moat omitted)

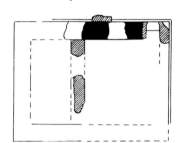

Plan of Ardamullivan Castle

Plan of Ardrahan Castle

ARDAMULLIVAN   R444951   B

Perched on a rock outcrop, this is a six storey tower measuring 10.8m by 6.9m built in two stages with vaults over the first and fourth levels in the east end and vaults over the first and fifth levels of the later western part. Prior to recent restoration it was complete except for the loss of most of the parapet and the east end gable. The SW and NE corners have square bartizans, and there are machicolations on the south wall of the eastern part and over east-facing entrance. The second and fourth storey rooms have wall paintings. The fireplaces in the SW corner of the western part at second and fifth storey level are insertions. Another fireplace inserted in the embrasure of a loop on the north side of the lowest level simply used the loop to let the smoke out. In 1579 Dermot O'Shaughnessy (who favoured the English) and his nephew John killed each other in a fight over possession of the castle. The local populace had supported John because of Dermot's betrayal of Dr Creagh, Archbishop of Armagh some years earlier.

ARDFRY   M347213

A platform 50m long by 25m wide was surrounded by a wet moat 3m wide. Only the western part still contains water, directly out of which rise the walls of the lowest level of a tower house 9.7m by 9m with just one double-splayed loop. One wall of a later wing adjoins to the north, with a fireplace in the angle between it and the tower.

ARDRAHAN   M461123   C

Lying in the SW part of a bawn about 30m by 40m enclosed by footings of a wall and a ditch 6m wide are the recently collapsed remains of the NW wall of a hall-keep measuring 17m by 12.5m, probably built by Maurice FitzGerald in the 1240s. More remains standing of a crosswall inserted into the keep in the later medieval period. One window high up served an added third storey in the SW end of the building, the rest of which was then still of just two low storeys.

ARKIN   L887073   B

An O'Brien tower here guarding the main harbour of Inis Mor was held in 1574 by James Lynch. In the 1650s the Cromwellian regime had it replaced by a rectangular fort built of stone taken from a nearby monastery, one of the surviving gunloops having an older cross-slab reused as a lintel. Nothing survives of two circular towers on the landward-facing south side, but one turret still remains together with a 60m long and 5m high section of the north wall and a watergate protected by a box-machicolation.

Bawn flanker at Aughnanure

Tower on Athenry town wall

Ardrahan Castle

North gateway of Athenry town wall

ATHENRY   M502277   E

The central keep begun c1235 by Meiler de Birmingham c1235 has recently been reroofed. It lies within the NW side of a bailey 50m by 40m still enclosed on the east and SW sides by a loopholed wall 1.1m thick above a wide battered base. It incorporates the outer wall of a hall block 24m long by 11m wide with circular towers 8m in diameter above their battered bases at either end. Neither tower projects much beyond the line of the curtain wall. A stair adjoined the northern tower, which is now reduced to its base. See page 5.

The keep measures 16.5m by 10.5m above a deeply battered base rising to first floor level. Each storeys has an entrance at the south end of the SE side, and an embrasure in the centre of each wall, the lower ones with mere slits but the upper ones with trefoil-headed lancets. The upper room also has a latrine at the northern corner and its doorway has finely carved capitals. Soon after completion the walls were raised to protect the roof and given a parapet with tall crossloops. In the 15th century a new roof and attic were created within this wall-walk and the former roof space become a windowless third storey, whilst in the lowest storey vaults were inserted upon a row of square piers.

The castle lies at the NE end of the town which has about half of its circuit of early 14th century walls remaining, with long stretches along the west and south sides, although much reduced in height and overgrown. Richard de Birmingham was one of the commanders of the English army which defeated and killed Felim O'Connor outside these walls in 1316. One tall slender circular tower also survives, and parts of four others. Of six gateways only the North Gate now remains. The town never occupied all the generous space within the walls and after it was sacked by the Earl of Clanricarde's sons in 1574 and 1577 a new southern wall was built to enclose the area actually developed. Athenry was again sacked in 1596 by Hugh O'Donnell and the castle seems to have been then left in ruins.

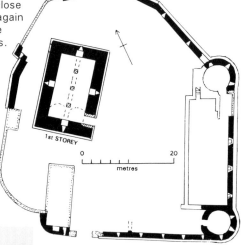

1st STOREY

0 20
metres

Plan of Athenry Castle

Upper doorway of keep at Athenry

Athenry Castle

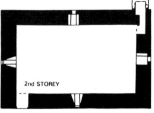

2nd STOREY

Athenry: plan of keep

AUGHNANURE   M152417 E

Beside the Drimneen River is one of the best preserved of the larger strongholds of the Irish chiefs. A modern hipped roof covers a six storey tower measuring 12.5m by 8.6m, rising 16.4m to the wall-walk, off which are four central box-machicolations, one of which commands the entrance in the east wall. This wall also has mural chambers, and a spiral stair, and square corner bartizans contain small rooms at the level of the lord's suite on the third storey. This level and the next two have mullioned windows. Much of the wall of the inner bawn 36m by 21m surrounding the tower stands on low cliffs. The vulnerable east and SE walls facing flat ground have been destroyed, leaving the stone-roofed SE corner flanker with gunloops (later used as a dovecote) now standing isolated. These sides are protected by an outer bawn roughly 50m square with three square turrets and a round flanker at the SE corner. The west side of this bawn was occupied by a hall of which there remains only the inner wall with fine carvings on the window embrasure soffits, the outer wall having fallen into a tributary river which has undermined it. In 1572 the castle was captured from the family of the O'Flaherty chief by Sir Edward Fitton, Governor of Connacht, and was handed over to Morogh O'Flaherty, one of a junior branch of the family enticed over to the English side. Although granted to the Earl of Clanricarde in the 17th century, the castle remained occupied by the O'Flahertys until the early 18th century, when it passed to Lord St George on the foreclosure of a mortgage.

Hall window

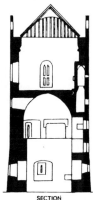

SECTION

Aughnanure: tower plan and section

Plan of Aughnanure Castle

Tower house at Aughnanure

Ballybroder Castle

Ballindooly Castle

BALLINASLOE   M858311   C

The modern house of Ivy Lodge by the River Suck lies within a bawn 50m by 54m with an ivy-mantled crenellated wall up to 5m high and a circular flanker with gunloops and an upper fireplace in the SW corner. The keystone dated 1597 with the name Anthony Braklon (or Brabazon), Governor of Connacht, lying east of the house has probably come from the gateway on the east side. Water courses supplying a corn mill flank the east and west walls whilst the north wall is now pierced at each end by modern doorways. Nothing remains of an older castle assumed to have stood on this site. It was founded by Turlough O'Connor in 1124 and rebuilt by the Normans in 1245. Tadhg O'Kelly is said to have erected a new castle in the 14th century which was later held by the Earl of Clanricarde until taken over by the English authorities in 1579. The bawn was held against General Ireton in 1651-2.

BALLINDERRY   M445462   C

There is a sheila-na-gig on the keystone of the pointed-headed entrance doorway in the east wall of this six storey tower which was held by John Burke in 1574. The four intermediate storeys all have fireplaces in the south wall and there are vaults over the second and fourth storey main rooms, whilst there are mural chambers in the east wall and a spiral stair in the NE corner. Latrines are provided in the north wall on the third storey and at an intermediate level between the third and fourth storeys. The third storey has remains of bartizans on the SE and NW corners and the top storey had a machicolation over the entrance. Some of the windows are of two lights, and some have ogival heads.

BALLINDOOLY   M315291   C

This restored tower lies by a road above Ballindooly Lough. There are three storeys under a vault and a fine upper storey and attic above it. A spiral stair in the east corner adjoins the entrance surmounted by mural chambers in the SE wall. The second storey has a latrine and a fireplace in the SW wall and there is a latrine on a level intermediate between the second and third storeys. A third latrine at fourth storey level has access in its floor to a hidden chamber in the haunch of the vault. This level has two-light windows in round-headed embrasures with decorated soffits.

BALLINDUFF   M306419

Thomas MacHenry held this tower in 1574. The east-facing entrance was blocked when a wing, now very ruinous, was added on this side. The tower has four storeys with vaults over both the cellar and the second storey, which has a latrine. The upper levels are linked by straight staircases. The summit has corbels for central machicolations on each wall.

BALLYBRIT   M334275

Only the end wall of the tower ever built, the SW side which was intended to be internal being of poorer quality masonry and having blocked doorways for the intended main rooms. The structure lies within a racecourse and contains the usual spiral stair and a tier of three upper chambers over a centrally located entrance passage. The third storey room has a fireplace and was vaulted. This tower was held by Redmund MacThomas in 1574.

BALLYBRODER   M652188   D

This tower measuring 10.3m by 8.2m has chambers over the entrance in the east end wall with a spiral stair in the NE corner. At the level of the vaulted third storey a passage in the north wall leading to a latrine from the staircase is almost blocked by the flue of a fireplace inserted below it into a second storey window embrasure.

BALLYDONNELLAN   M723223   D

The western half of a tower about 13m by 10m stands four storeys high with a chimney stack with two string courses. The lowest level contained two vaulted rooms, but the eastern one is now either filled in or buried under a pile of rubble. The tower later became a wing of a 17th century house 26m long by 11m wide of which only footings remain, although the shell remains of a four storey wing built to balance it at the other end in the 18th century by the O'Donellan family. Also probably of that period is the stone now at Aughrim School recording the building of the old tower in 1412 by Tully O'Donellan. A second O'Donnellan tower once stood in the adjoining townland of Ballydonnellan West.

Ballybroder: plans

Ballindooly: plan

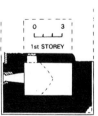

Ballydonellan: plan

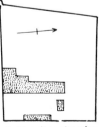

Ballinasloe: site plan

Ballydonellan Castle

BALLYLEE   M481062   E

This 16th century tower measuring about 9.5m by 8.5m beside a stream is best known because it was restored and inhabited by the poet W.B.Yeats in the 1920s. Original two-light windows with transoms survive in the fifth storey over a vaulted loft but larger new windows have been inserted in the lower storeys. The spiral stair lies in the SW corner, beside the west-facing entrance now within a later wing. By the 1930s the tower was derelict again but it was later restored to serve as a Yeats museum.

BALLYLIN   M508161

This tower measuring 8.6m by 7.8m with its upper features hidden in ivy has a damaged entrance on the east, a spiral stair in the NE corner and a latrine chute in the NW corner.

BALLYMAQUIFF   M450096   D

There are two vaults in this tower measuring 10.4m by 8.6m set on a low rock but the topmost level has been destroyed. At the upper vault level there is a latrine in the NW wall and a chamber in the NE wall, whilst the second storey main room has a fireplace. A very large window embrasure below the latter and set over the entrance may have served as an oratory. The staircase in the north corner has a loop from its base piercing the western jamb of the entrance, and an angleloop higher up. There is no evidence of a floor for a loft under the lower vault, although there is a doorway for access onto such a floor.

BALLYMORE   M879200

The fourth and fifth storeys of this inhabited tower have windows of two or three lights. The fourth storey has a bartizan on the SW corner and there are bartizans at wall-walk level on the NW and SE corners. The entrance faces east into a later house built by the Seymour family which also adjoins the north side of the tower. John Lawrence is said to have built the tower after marrying an O'Madden heiress in 1585. The castle was granted to Sir Thomas Newcomen in the 1650s and was sold to the Eyres c1720.

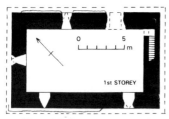

Plan of Ballynacourty Castle

Ballymaquiff Castle

Interior of hall-house at Ballynacourty

Ballylee Castle

Ballymore Castle

SECTION

0   3
metres

2nd STOREY

1st STOREY

1st STOREY

Plan of Ballymulfaig Castle

0   10
metres

Ballylin: plan

Ballymaquiff:
plans & section

BALLYMULFAIG   M402019

Beside a farm is a 50m long section of the south wall of a bawn with a 6m diameter SW flanker and a central projection (breached by a track) both well-provided with gunloops.

BALLYNABANABA   M745345

This O'Mullally tower now stands three storeys high but part of the east side has fallen and the north wall containing the latrines is badly cracked. There was a spiral stair in the NE corner. The third storey has a fireplace in the west wall. Some of the loops are ogival-headed. A 7m high motte with a summit 15m across lies by the road to the NW.

BALLYNACOURTY   M364185   D

This hall-house measures 16.8m by 10.3m over walls 1.6m thick above a battered base, the lower part of which has been robbed. The lower level has five loops, all defaced, and a stair leading up in the SE end wall to an upper storey of which little remains. The castle is assumed to have been built by the de Burghs in the mid 13th century and in 1574 was held by William MacRichard.

BALLYNAHINCH   L762480   I

Donell Ecowga held this tower on an island in Ballynahinch Lake in 1574, and he is reputed to have built it from materials taken from Toombeola Abbey. Of four storeys and measuring 9m long up to 7m wide, it was much altered in the 18th century when a wing containing kilns was added on the west side. A spiral stair in the SE corner adjoins the east-facing entrance. The second storey has a latrine in the south wall.

Bawn at Blindwell

Barnaderg Castle

BALLYNAHIVNIA   M557208   C

The lowest level of this tower measuring 11m by 9m has three gunloops in the form of horizontal slots set in embrasures, whilst the second storey has ogival-headed loops, the third storey has angle-loops, and the fourth storey is vaulted. The damaged entrance lies in the east side and the spiral stair lies in the SE corner.

BANAGHER   M004159   B

This much altered building on the west bank of the River Shannon remained in military use until the 19th century. One or both of the circular towers of 5.4m and 6.5m respective diameters at the eastern corners of a main block 12.4m by 9.8m may be additions.

BARNADERG   M516484   C

The south end wall containing the entrance, staircase and mural chambers of this late 16th century O'Kelly tower measuring 9.2m by 7.8m has fallen. The surviving walls have corbels for central machicolations. Including an attic within the roof there were five storeys without either vaults or internal offsets to carry floor beams. The fireplaces in the east wall must be insertions since that at second storey level blocks an ogival-headed loop, and that on the fourth storey blocks a two-light window with a transom. One loop in the lowest level is flanked by gunloops. The tower stands on a 1.5m high platform 55m long by 24m wide.

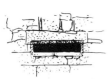

Ballynahivnia: gunloop

Barnaderg: plan

Plans of Ballynahivnia Castle

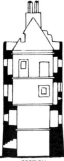

SECTION

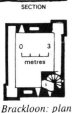

0   3
metres

Brackloon: plan

Ballynahivnia Castle

Brackloon Castle

BLINDWELL   M341595

The bawn here preserves much of its wall 1.5m thick and up to 4.5m high on the NE side around a court about 35m square. On the south side is a small projecting gateway. The gateway on the east side is not ancient, and the steps just south of it look later also. The SW corner of the stable-block within is ancient or is built of old materials.

BRACKLOON   M951190   C

The only vaults in this 16th century tower measuring 8.3m by 6.3m are in the tier of rooms over the entrance in a thick end wall also containing the entrance defended by a fourth storey box-machicolation and the spiral staircase. Most of the parapet survives around an attic within the roof gables, and there are square bartizans with numerous gunloops at two diagonally opposite corners. The walls are considerably thinner above the floor level of the third storey. The castle was captured in 1557 by the Lord Justice in his campaign against the
O'Conors of Offaly.

Cromwell's Castle, Banagher

Interior of Cahererillan Castle showing secret room

Caherakilleen Castle

Cahererillan Castle

KEEP

0   10

metres

GATEWAY

Plan of Caherakilleen Castle

Caherkinmonwee: plans

Cahererillan: plans & section

CAHERERILLAN   M372070 D

The 3.6m wide eastern part of this five storey O'Heyne tower measuring 8.6m by 8m was built first and contains mural chambers over the entrance and guard room and a spiral stair in the SE corner. Both the guard room and stair have loops penetrating the doorway jambs and there is a NE corner angle loop at second storey level. The added part has a latrine in the north wall. The vault over the cellar and its loft survives but another higher up has fallen, thus revealing to view the chamber hidden in its northern haunch, which was accessed though a hatch in a recess off a window embrasure above. See photo page 23.

CAHERGLASSAUN   M413065

There is a damaged entrance in the east wall of this O'Heyne tower measuring 9.2m by 8.4m with a latrine chute on the north side and a spiral stair in the NE corner. The lowest level is rather defaced inside. The second storey is vaulted and has a fireplace with a joggled lintel in the south wall which has been inserted into the embrasure of an ogival-headed loop. Other loops at this level were later replaced by mullioned windows. The castle was wrecked by an earthquake in 1755.

Caherglassaun Castle

Caherkinmonwee Castle

CAHERKINMONWEE   M536209   D

There are bartizans on all four corners of this tower measuring 10.4m by 9m. which was held by Myler Henry Burke in 1574 and has recently been reroofed, although work on a parapets is still proceeding. A stone loose on the site is lightly scratched with the date 1671 and the initials W.B. The second, third and fourth storeys all have latrines in the SW corner, the uppermost having an angle-loop. The spiral stair lies in the SE corner and there are two levels of rooms over the entrance in the east wall. The third storey has a vault with a north-south axis and the fourth and fifth storeys both form single large rooms with later fireplaces. An outbuilding to the south incorporates part of a bawn wall.

CAHERAKILLEEN   M553233

The buried base and two higher fragments of the sidewalls remain of a 13th century hall keep 14.4m long by 9.8m wide, together with part of a thinly walled added turret at the SE end. The keep lies on the NE side of a bawn roughly 30m square enclosed by a ditch and a wall 1.5m thick mostly reduced to its base, except for a fragment on the SE side adjoining a gateway with a drawbar slot. A fragment remains of one wall of an outbuilding on the SW side of the bawn. To the NE lie traces of various other buildings.

0   5
⌞ ⌞ ⌞ ⌞ ⌟ m

Plan of Castle Daly

CAHERNAMUCK   M608197

In the SE corner of a ditched platform are remains of a tower about 10m by 9m, part of the south end wall being 3m high. A turret about 4.5m by 6m clasping the NE corner stood four storeys high with vaults over the first and third levels until it was blown up by the landowner in 1991. The castle was held in 1574 by Walter Burke.

Caherglassaun: plan

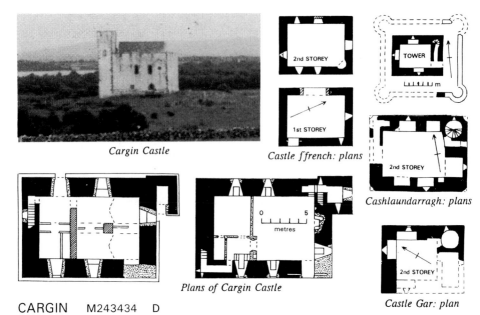

Cargin Castle

Castle ffrench: plans

2nd STOREY

1st STOREY

TOWER

Cashlaundarragh: plans

2nd STOREY

Plans of Cargin Castle

2nd STOREY

Castle Gar: plan

CARGIN   M243434   D

This 13th century hall-house measuring 14.7m by 10.5m with walls up to 2m thick over a battered plinth was restored in the 1970s. Most of the outer openings date from then, along with the whole of the south corner and the parapets. The lowest level now has an entrance on the NE side, close to where a service stair leads up in the NW wall, but originally there seems to have been a lower entrance below the doorway with draw-bar slots surviving at the south end of the SW wall of the upper storey. The stair up to the wall-walk is at the east corner where there is a three storey latrine turret 4m wide projecting 2.5m from the SE wall. In the later medieval period the lower storey was subdivided into two rooms, the largest of which has a two bay arcade with a central pier to support vaults. The upper storey has five window embrasures with seats and may also then have had the NW end divided off as a private chamber, although the existing subdividing walls are modern. The castle was held by William Gaynard in 1574.

CASHLAUNDARRAGH or RYEHILL   M524391

In 1574 this four storey tower measuring 11m by 8.4m was held by Ullick Lynch. A hole in the east wall represents the entrance, with a murder-hole over its lobby. The spiral stair in the NE corner now only rises to the second storey, which is vaulted and has a fireplace in the south wall and a latrine in the north wall. Only traces remain of various outbuildings and a bawn wall closely surrounding the tower, but there are low fragments of a circular SE flanker 4.3m in diameter and indications of another at the NE corner.

CASTLECREEVY   M327389

Now named after Croabh Ni Burke, this overgrown bawn on a rock outcrop may be the castle of "Yowghvle" noted in 1574 as a possession of John Lynch. The bawn measures 40m by 32m and has a fragmentary, ivy-covered wall up to 4m high, little of which remains on the north side. On the south side a possibly later building backs onto a D-shaped flanker 6m in diameter and there are other turrets on the NE and SE. On the east are traces of building beside a ball-alley built beside the bawn wall.

CASTLE DALY   M520091   D

A Blake tower originally known as Corbally has become part of the show facade of an 18th century house of the Dalys. This house has been destroyed apart from the wall linking the old tower to a second wing making a balanced composition completed by 19th century battlements. The old tower is actually just the much altered 5m wide end wall containing the entrance, mural chambers and staircase of an intended tower 8.8m wide.

CASTLE FFRENCH   M763453

A plaque with the ffrench family arms and the date 1683 is set in the SW wall of a four storey tower so as to block a small loop. It has probably come from a former outbuilding or bawn gateway but the tower itself may not be much earlier. It measures 8m by 6.2m over walls just 0.8m thick and the only defensive feature is the machicolation over the blocked east-facing entrance. There are no vaults or stairs and the second and third storeys have fireplaces in the NE and NW corners respectively. The tower looks like an estate official's lodging rather than a landed family's seat, and the main house itself may have been 200m further west where there are traces of a possible older tower and bawn. The estate belonged to the O'Kellys before it passed to the ffrench family.

CASTLEGAR   M320280   D

Parts of this tower held in 1574 by Roland Skerrit still stand four storeys high but only half remains of the SE wall which contained mural chambers over the entrance and a spiral stair in the east corner, and not much remains of a chamber in the SW haunch of the vault over the third storey. At the level of this vault a passage from the stair to a latrine led past a circular gunloop and a north-facing angle-loop.

Castle Daly

Castle Gar

Castle ffrench

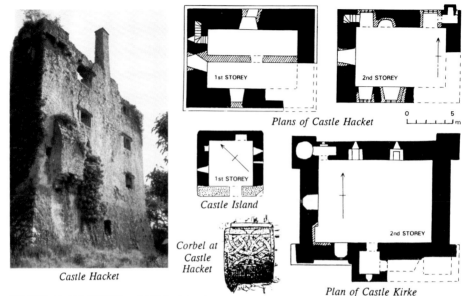

Plans of Castle Hacket

Castle Island

Corbel at Castle Hacket

Castle Hacket

Plan of Castle Kirke

CASTLE HACKET   M357492 G

This 13th century hall-house held by Ullick MacReamon Burke in 1585 measures 13.4m by 9.8m above a deeply battered base. The longitudinal crosswall carrying vaults over two cellars is an insertion blocking an original loop at the west end. A service stair in the NW corner connects the two lowest levels. The third and fourth storeys provided in a late 16th century remodelling were reached either by wooden internal stairs or by a staircase in the destroyed SE corner, beside which must have been the entrance. The second storey has a latrine projecting on the north side and a fireplace in the north wall, and the upper levels have fireplaces in the west end wall, chimney stacks remaining above both positions. All these levels have remains of windows of two or three lights with hoodmoulds. Much of the parapet remains, with square bartizans on the SW and NE corners. Ornately carved corbels carried the beams of the floor of third storey. Only the roof-mark remains of a later block adjoining the east wall, the castle having remained occupied until 1703.

CASTLE ISLAND   R473987

Hidden in foliage on an island in Lough Cultra is a tower 7.1m square over walls 1.1m thick which in 1574 was held by the Earl of Clanricarde's son John. The lowest level has a fine shouldered-linteled fireplace and an entrance in the rebuilt SW wall opposite. Only one upper storey survives, with evidence of bartizans on the east and west corners.

CASTLE KIRKE   L996502 D

In 1233 Felim O'Connor, King of Connacht burnt a castle here built in 1232. The existing hall-house on an island in Lough Corrib was probably built c1235. It measures 16m by 13m over walls 2m thick with projecting corner turrets. A forebuilding in the middle of the south side contains an upper entrance reached by a set of external steps with a portcullis groove at the bottom. A spiral stair in the NW turret leads down to a lower storey now full of debris but appearing to have a latrine and loops with seats in the embrasures with rere-arches like those above. In the 16th century the O'Flahertys, then owners, provided the lower level with its own entrance doorway (now blocked) with a circular gunport near it.

CASTLE TAYLOR   M466141 D

The vault over the lowest storey of this tower has been altered, probably when the adjoining house was added, and the belfry on the parapet may also be of that period. The entrance lies in the NW wall and the spiral stair lies in the north corner. At second storey level a passage in the NE wall leads from the stair to the main room and then on past a loop in the east corner to steps down to a room in the vault haunch. The third storey loops are ogival-headed. The castle was held by the Taylor family until 1825.

CLAREGALWAY   M373333 C

There is portcullis groove in the pointed-headed SE-facing entrance of this fine tower measuring 12.3m by 10.2m built in the 15th century by the Clanricarde Burkes. Originally the tower contained a lowest room with five loops in deep embrasures, a lofty vaulted room above for the lord with a fireplace and latrine in the SW wall and a passage in the NE wall, and a hall on top with two-light windows on all four sides, three of them having small rooms adjoining their embrasures. The circular gunloop near the foot of the stair in the east corner must be a later insertion. Either originally or as a later alteration a loft was created under the vault, with access though a doorway knocked through from the uppermost of two large mural chambers over the entrance, the lowest level having an arcade of two arches to widen the wall internally to contain these chambers. The upper mural chamber has a fireplace and latrine. Each of the NE and NW sides has one cross-loop. A loft also seems to have later been inserted within the hall roof space. Parts of the parapets remain, with corbels for a machicolation over the entrance and centrally placed machicolations on each of the other sides.

Claregalway: section

0   10

metres

4TH STOREY

2ND STOREY

2nd STOREY

Castle Taylor: plan

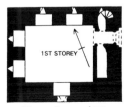

1ST STOREY

Claregalway: plans

Castle Taylor

CLOGHBALLYMORE   M399140

The fifth storey of this tall, narrow tower has mullion-and-transom windows, above which are corbels of former central machicolations, the original parapet having been replaced by a level-topped one. There is an angle-loop in the NE corner and a latrine on the south side, whilst there is a later house on the north side.

CLOGHAREVAUN   M582243   C

Fragments still complete to the wall-walk and parapet still remain of the west wall of a bawn 46m by 30m. On the east side, overlooking the river, are remains of a tower house 7m wide and probably once about 8.5m long. The north end wall has an entrance and mural chambers at second and third storey levels. Both the main room and mural room at third storey level were vaulted, and the 4th storey formed one large room, with one ogival-headed north loop still surviving.

CLOGHASTOOKEEN   M565176   C

Just north of a cemetery are traces of a polygonal bawn 45m across with the lower parts of the north and east walls of a tower about 11m by 9m on the east side. The north wall contained the entrance. In 1574 the castle was held by the MacEdmund MacUllick Burkes.

CLOGHAUN   M537108

This is the restored north end wall of a tower, the main body of which was never built. It contains chambers over an entrance passage protected by a machicolation and a spiral stair in the eastern part, and is now surrounded by a modern bawn about 19m square.

CLOGHROAK   M492144   C

This Burke tower measuring 8.1m by 7.1m has an arch over the east end of the second storey room to carry a passage from the spiral stair in the NE corner to a latrine in the SE corner. Nothing remains of the top room over the third storey vault. The entrance faces north to where there was a bawn and where there are still extensive garden walls. Of the bawn there remain only that part which formed the south wall of a range extending 25m west of the tower, plus a short low section beyond.

Cloghroak Castle

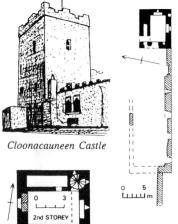

Cloonacauneen Castle

2nd STOREY

Cloghroak: plans

CLONBROCK   M744397

Hidden in dense vegetation by the Clonbrock River lie a tower about 13m by 11m and three circular towers 6m diameter which lay at the corners of the bawn. The east-facing entrance has a yett, possibly original. From it a stair rises to where a spiral stair rises from the second to the fourth storey in the SE corner. A second stair in the SW corner then rises to the fifth and sixth storeys and the wall-walk, where there is a string course at the base of the parapet. There are mural chambers in the south wall and latrines in the north wall. The 3rd storey has fireplaces in both the east and west walls, and there are other fireplaces on the second storey in the east wall and on the 4th storey in the west wall. There are windows of two and three lights with hoodmoulds in the upper levels. The doorways in the lowest levels of the west wall led to an added wing now destroyed.

CLOONACAUNEEN   M342307   H

A four storey tower held by Richard Burke in 1574 measuring 9.5m by 7.5m and a 19th century house added against the south side were restored from ruin in the 1960s. A spiral stair in the SE corner adjoins the east-facing entrance with mural chambers over it. The fourth storey has a fireplace in the north wall and a latrine, the latter having access in its floor to a hidden chamber in the south haunch of the third storey vault. The second storey also has a north fireplace and there is a gallery passage between this level and the third storey to a latrine. Some of the windows are of two ogival-headed lights.

CLOONBOO   N328370   D

This ivy-covered four storey tower measuring 11.6m by 10.2m was held by Moyler MacShean in 1574. The lowest level is vaulted and has an entrance on the north side, where there are corbels for a former machicolation. The second storey has a fireplace at the south end and a latrine on the east, whilst the third storey has a chamber in the SE corner and steps in the NE and SW corners down to rooms in the haunches of the vault. See page 6.

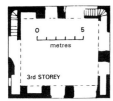

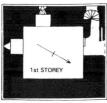

Plans of Cloonboo Castle   *Interior of Cloonboo Castle*

Cregg Castle

Corrofin Castle

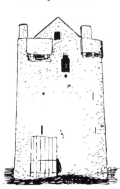

Cloondagauv Castle

Plans of Corrofin Castle

CLOONDAGAUV   R806997

This Burke tower beside Lough Derg is now owned by a branch of that family living in America. It is roofed but empty and has a damaged entrance and stair in the south end wall. The spiral stair has a crossloop at second storey level and the fifth storey room has windows of two and three lights with transoms and hoodmoulds, whilst at the top there are chimney stacks on the east and west sides and bartizans with the outer angle canted off upon the NW and SE corners and a machicolation over the entrance.

CORROFIN   M426433   C

A tower measuring 11m by 9.8m lies in the south corner of a platform 40m square near the River Clare. The Annals of the Four Masters record its construction in 1451 by Lord Clanricarde, and it was held by Richard Burke in 1585. The entrance on the NE side has grooves for a portcullis and a passage to a staircase in the east corner. There are vaults over the first and third of four storeys and the second storey has a latrine in the SE wall, whilst the third storey has a fireplace on the NW side. Of the fourth storey only a fragment remains on the SW side. There are indications that a building adjoined the NW side. The SW side has corbels for a central machicolation.

Cloondagauv: plan

CREGBOYNE   M389417   G

Footings of a house 12m long by 6m wide lie in the centre of a bawn 67m by 48m enclosed by a wall 1.5m thick and 1.8m high with a gateway on the east side. At the NW and SE corners are circular flankers 4.6m in diameter with two storeys each with five gunloops. A latrine nearby in the south wall served a former building in this corner.

Cloondagauv Castle

Creggmulgrany Castle

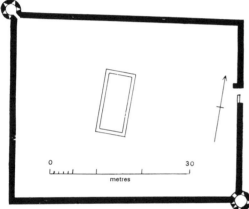

0   30
metres

Plan of bawn at Cregboyne

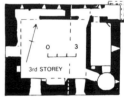

0   3

3rd STOREY

Creggmulgrany: plan

CREGG   M357375   H

A four storey tower built by the Kirwans in 1648 survives in a much altered form as the central part of a later mansion. All the features on the show side to the south are modern but a blocked doorway and windows with hoodmoulds survive in the north wall.

CREGGANNA   M394214

The tower was occupied until the late 18th century and has consequently been modernised. The second storey is vaulted. The east wall contains the entrance and a tier of rooms above, two of which have ogival-headed loops. These rooms are on different levels to the main rooms.

CREGGMULGRANY   M151152   C

Joins in the north and south walls indicate that the lower part of the east wall containing a tier of chambers of the entrance and the SE corner spiral stair was built first. The vaulted lowest storey of the rest was added to it, then a wider upper section of the east wall was built with an arch over the main rooms to support a passage from the stair to a latrine in the north wall. Finally the rest of the main body was added, resulting in a six storey structure measuring 12.4m by 9.6m with a tier of fireplaces in the west wall, although the defaced fireplace of the second storey is in the south wall. A bartizan with gunloops at third storey level on the NE corner is represented by little more than a gaping hole. There are traces of a surrounding bawn wall. This tower was held in 1574 by Shane Roewgh.

CUMMER   M406466   D

A wall 1.2m thick above a battered base surrounds a bawn about 30m across which was square at the south corner, where only footings remain, but polygonal on the NW side, also reduced to footings, and on the NE where two long fragments stand 3m high. There may have been a flanker facing north. On the west, guarding the bawn gateway, is the 4m high inner wall, with traces of a vault, of a tower about 8.7m by 6.3m. This castle was held by Ullick MacRichard in 1574 and was wrecked by Cromwell in the 1650s after resistance by the then occupants, the O'Shaughnessys.

DEERPARK   M546132   C

This is the SE end wall of a MacHubert Burke tower, the main body of which was never built. It measures 8.2m by 4.2m and contains a spiral stair and a tier of three rooms, the topmost vaulted, over an entrance passage with a drawbar slot and a small guard room.

DERRYDONNELL   M452252

A fragmentary later house projects out from the NE side of a bawn 17m by 16m with spear-head shaped flankers with gunloops at the east and west corners and an entrance with a drawbar slot facing NW. The 1m thick bawn wall surrounds a tower 11m by 9.4m with five levels of small rooms over an entrance passage on the NE and a spiral stair in the north corner. The almost square second storey main room has a passage leading around the west corner to a latrine in the SW wall. The lowest main room is full of rubble. Just one corbel remains of a central machicolation on the NW side. The tower existed by 1574 when it was held by Tybbot McAwgl, but it was held by Ullick Burke, 3rd Earl of Clanricarde at his death in 1608, and he may have added the bawn.

Dungory: plan

Cummer Castle

Derrydonnell Castle

Deerpark Castle

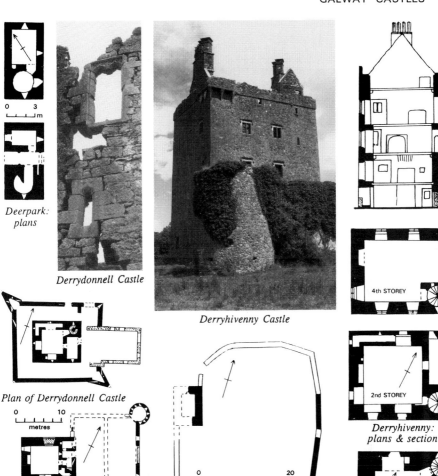

Deerpark:
plans

Derrydonnell Castle

Derryhivenny Castle

4th STOREY

Plan of Derrydonnell Castle

2nd STOREY

Derryhivenny:
plans & section

Plan of Derryhivenny Castle Plan of Cummer Castle

3rd STOREY

DERRYHIVENNY M872085 A

Derrydonnell: plan

A wall 0.9m thick with diagonally opposite corner flankers 4.5m in diameter encloses a bawn 18.4m by 13m in front of the doorway of a tower 11.9m by 9.7m, and also encloses a space 4.4m wide beside the south wall. Much of the bawn seems to have been filled by an outbuilding along the east side. One flanker has a corbel inscribed with the year 1643 and the initials of Daniel O'Madden but the tower may be slightly older. It rises 14m to the wall-walk and contains five low unvaulted storeys with a tier of mural chambers over the entrance passage, which is dog-leg shaped and commanded by a loop from the lowest room, with a gunloop opening off the straight passage to the foot of the spiral stair in the east corner. The third storey has a latrine and fireplace, whilst the fourth storey has one big chamber with a fireplace and six mullioned windows, that at the NE end being of three lights. At the top there are square bartizans on the SW and NE corners.

DERRYMACLAUGHNA   M445376   D

This tower measuring 11.6m by 8.4m was held by John Burke in 1574. A spiral stair in the NW corner adjoins a west-facing entrance, above which are four upper levels of mural chambers. The second and fourth storeys have fireplaces in the east wall and the fifth storey has a fireplace on the south, whilst the third storey has remains of a vault with a passage in its northern haunch. Some of the upper windows are of two lights with ogival heads or three lights with a hoodmoulding. Only a roof mark remains of a later range to the west. The bulged NE corner is a result of an attempt to blow up the tower. See p9.

DRUMHARSNA   M436106   B

Shane Ballagh held this tower measuring 9.6m by 8.3m in 1574. There are vaults over the second and fourth storeys and the fifth storey was partly in the roof with wall-walks on parts of the sidewalls only. A machicolation commands the entrance, which lies in the east wall, and has in conjunction with it a tier of mural chambers and a spiral stair in the SE corner. The upper parts have seen a number of alterations, fireplaces having been inserted into loops on the north side of the first, third and fourth storeys.

Dungory Castle

DUNKELLIN   M441183

Low corners and footings remain of a building about 12.5m by 10.8m with a longitudinal crosswall and a surrounding ditch. Possibly founded in the 13th century by Jordan de Exeter, it was the seat of a barony created or recreated in 1585.

Dunmore Castle

Drumharsna Castle

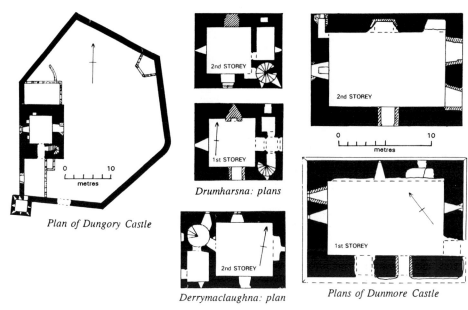

Plan of Dungory Castle

Drumharsna: plans

Derrymaclaughna: plan

Plans of Dunmore Castle

DUNGORY   M380511   E

The O'Hynes' 16th century tower with machicolations in the centre of each face stands on the west side of a hexagonal bawn 35m across set on a mound by Kinvarra Bay. The tower measures 11.6m by 9.8m and has four storeys and an attic. The third storey has a two-light window in the middle of each side, the southern window having a very wide embrasure off which there is a doorway to a chamber in the SW corner, and there is a fireplace in the NW corner. As rebuilt in 1642 the bawn wall is 1.2m thick and rises 2.7m to a wall-walk protected by a parapet 2m high with gunloops. A four-gabled SW corner turret flanks the south gateway. The castle later passed to the Martins of Tullira. The tower has been reroofed and is used for staging medieval banquets. Two low modern wings adjoin it. Part of a vault remains of a second tower to the SW at 379104 (see p63).

DUNMORE   M500640   A

Dunmore was given by the de Burghs to Meilor de Birmingham in the 1220s and was held by the Birminghams until their forfeiture in the 1650s. Occupied until the 19th century, the keep lies within an enclosure 64m by 30m which may represent a fort built in the early 12th century by Turlough O'Connor and there are remains of a gateway on the east side. There is a reference in 1280 to a now vanished town wall under construction. The keep has seen much alteration and repair over the years, having been burnt by the O'Connors in 1249 and 1315, and by the O'Flynns in 1284, whilst it was captured by Sir Henry Sidney in the 1570s. It measures 16.4m by 11.8m above a tall battered base and originally contained just one upper chamber over a basement. One of the loops of the original parapet was later used as a third storey window and in its present form, as reconstructed c1575-1600, the building had four unvaulted storeys plus an attic within the roof gables, upon which are chimneystacks. The east gable lies within the wall-walk and parapet. The second storey has a fireplace on the north, a latrine in the NW corner and an entrance doorway in the east wall. A second entrance was later inserted below it. The third storey with mullion-and-transom windows facing south was subdivided, having fireplaces in both north and east walls. The attic has a fireplace at the west end.

Dunmore Castle

Doorway at Feartagar

DUNSANDLE   M580218

This MacHubert Burke tower hidden in woods was held by the Daly family from the 18th century until recently. Now restored by a new owner, it measures 12.6 by 8.3m and has an entrance in the east wall with a passage to a spiral stair in the NE corner, this end being raised up higher than the rest. The original outer doorway has been transferred to the south side, facing towards where there are fragments of a later wing. The tower contains an unusual groin-vault and has angle loops in the northern corners and central machicolations on each side. It lies on the west side of a bawn 22m by 18m enclosed (except for a wide breach on the north) by a loopholed wall 1m thick with a NW corner flanker 4m square furnished with gunloops, one of which (recently restored) pierces the SW angle to cover the (restored) entrance arch between here and the main tower. The added wing projected south of the bawn and has traces of adjoining rooms built out beyond the bawn wall. A later ice-house adjoins the bawn NE corner.

FARTAMORE   M393588   C

A very ruinous tower 11.6m by 9.2 now lacking its north corner containing the NE-facing entrance lies in the south corner of a bawn about 32m square of which the west side still stands 2m high. The tower second storey, which appears to have once had a rare groin-vault, has a passage to a latrine in the south corner.

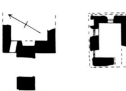

Castle Ellen
(see page 61)

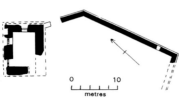

Plan of Fartamore Castle

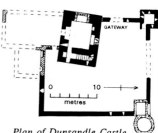

Plan of Dunsandle Castle

Dunsandle Castle

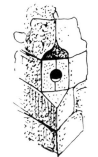

Restored angle-gunloop at Dunsandle

FEARTAGAR   M376581   B

The alternative name of Jenning's Castle is anglicised from Eion, the first name of several successive Burke owners. The tower measures 11.8m by 9.6m and has a pointed-headed entrance doorway in the east wall. From it stairs lead south to a spiral stair in the SE corner. There is a mural room over the entrance and the main room at that level is vaulted and has an additional service stair leading down around the NW corner. The three topmost storeys have just one single large chamber, although there is a chamber on the south side formed in the haunch of the vault. The third storey has a latrine in the north wall. The north wall is surmounted by the chimney stack of fireplaces at the second, third and fourth storey levels, the middle one being an insertion blocking the embrasure of a window of two lights with ogival heads. There is also a fifth storey fireplace in the west wall, where there is a stack upon the gable. All four corners have circular bartizans, that at the NE corner adjoining a machicolation over the doorway. A covered well lies near the south side.

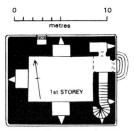

Plan of Feartagar Castle

Feartagar Castle

Fartamore Castle

Bartizan at Feartagar

Fiddaun Castle

Furmina Castle

Town wall at Galway

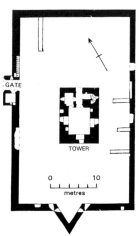

Plan of Fiddaun Castle

FIDDAUN   R410958   D

The last O'Shaughnessy to reside here fled to France in 1697. The tower measures 11.7m by 8.7m and had seven storeys, including an attic within the wall-walk, the third storey having bartizans at the north and south corners. The second and fifth storeys are vaulted and have passages to latrines on the NW side. The north and west corners have angle-loops. The tower lies inside a bawn 39m long by 24m wide with walls mostly 1.5m thick with a salient flanker in the middle of the west end, a rectangular two storey gatehouse on the north, and a postern on the south. There are traces of former lean-to buildings and a latrine chute at the SW corner. Only the gatehouse remains of an outer bawn.

FURMINA   L982023   C

This hall-house on Inisheer is known locally as Caislean Ui Brien and probably dates from the 14th century. Held in 1574 by Dominick Lynch, it measures 13.2m by 7.6m and is now entered by a later opening below the original upper entrance in the NE wall, which is flanked by beam holes for external wooden stairs. On the upper level the SW wall contains a trefoil-headed loop and a stair to the wall-walk and the now-fragmentary parapet. One corbel remains of a bartizan at the north corner. The basement, later divided into three vaulted rooms, seems to have only been entered from above.

Blake's Castle, Galway

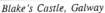

Lynch's Castle, Galway

GALWAY   M299252 B   &   M 297250 B

The tower of c1500 known as Lynch's Castle after the town's leading family bears their arms plus those of Henry VII and the Earl of Kildare, then Lord Deputy. No less than 84 members of the Lynch family served as mayor of the town between 1485 and 1654. The tower has gargoyles, a rarity in Ireland, and windows with particularly ornate ends to the hoodmoulds. The windows themselves now have sashes. In 1966 the tower was adapted as a branch office of the Munster and Leinster bank. The facade of a tower known as Blake's Castle on the north side of the Fish Market in the SW corner of the town is the only relic of many other such urban tower houses shown on a map of 1651. This tower has trefoil-headed loops set either side of the east corner at second storey level and a machicolation over the entrance. It served as the county jail from 1686 until 1810.

Nothing remains of a castle beside the river built by Richard de Burgh in 1232, and destroyed by Felim O'Connor in 1233, but there are remains of the town walls begun in the 1270s. They survive mostly on the NW and SW sides towards the River Corrib, where there were a series of quays. The so-called Spanish Arch and the adjoining length of wall with a corbelled parapet may be part of the new defences here built in the 1490s. After the town was captured by the Burkes and O'Briens in 1504 a new ditch was created on the east side. The west gate bore the date 1549 and inscription recording its construction as a protection against the "ferocious O'Flaherties", traditional enemies of the English-speaking townsfolk loyal to the Crown. In the 17th century the most vulnerable NE end was strengthened by a new outer wall with arrowhead-shaped bastions in the middle and at the corners. Excavations have revealed the base of the NE bastion. The Cromwellian commander Sir Charles Coote besieged the town by land and sea for nine months until it surrendered in April 1652. The earthwork forts with spearhead-shaped corner bastions still partly remaining at M305263 and M302250 formed part of an outer ring of defences of this period. The town was devastated again during the wars of 1689-91.

GARBALLY   M578398   C

This tower 8.7m wide existed by 1504 when MacWilliam de Burgo destroyed it and two other O'Kelly castles. The NE wall remains complete to the lower part of the parapet together with most of the adjoining NW and SE walls, the latter containing the pointed-headed entrance doorway recessed within an outer arch allowing an extra murder-hole in addition to the usual one over the lobby. A straight stair rises towards where there was a spiral stair in the south corner. There was a vault over the second storey, where the NW wall contains a passage, above which is a mural chamber. Corbels for machicolations remain on the NE and SE walls. One upper window is of two lights with ogival heads.

GLINSK   M715670   A

Ullick Burke is thought to have built this stronghouse after he was created a baronet in 1628. It measures 22.6m by 13.3m over walls mostly 1.7m thick, although the east and west walls are 1.6m thick since they contain tiers of fireplaces rising to chimney stacks set diagonally in rows of five. The western part of the low basement with narrow windows flanked by gunloops was a kitchen with a wide fireplace with an oven. Above were three storeys of upper rooms with mullion-and-transom windows of two and three lights. The dividing walls and central staircase were of wood. The main entrance was at second storey level on the south side where the centre is recessed to give the effect of two wide wings each of which has a square bartizan on the outermost corner, the doorway being into the east side of the west wing. The south side faced a bawn of which the west wall and the base of the circular SE flanker remains. A third machicolation commanded a back doorway with a flanking gunloop on the north side. In the wall base just east of this doorway is a reset fragment of an ogival-headed loop from an earlier castle on or near this site which belonged to Hubert MacDavy Burke in 1574.

Garbally: plan

Glinsk Castle

Plan of Glinsk Castle

Garbally Castle

Isert Kelly Castle

GRANGE EAST   M430344

Not much remains of the south and west walls of this Burke tower above the vault over the lowest of four storeys, and there are only traces of a third storey vault. Stairs lead up to where a spiral stair begins in the NE corner at second storey level. The third storey has a passage in the east wall and a latrine in the NW corner. Running northwards for 8m from this corner is part of a bawn wall ending with a ruinous arched opening.

ISERT KELLY   M520121   B

The third storey main room lies over a vault and has an inserted fireplace dated 1604 with the initials W.H. The tower measures 13.5m by 11m, stands 21m high to the top of the corner turrets and lies within a large flanker at the SW corner of a bawn about 60m square represented by footings of its wall and a large outbuilding in the SE corner, plus traces of the surrounding wet moat. The lowest level of the tower has crossloops and the second storey has mullioned windows. The castle belonged to the MacHuberts and then passed to the MacRedmonds, both branches of the Burke clan.

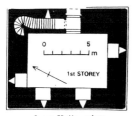

Isert Kelly: plan

KILCLOONEY   M423605

The lowest two storeys covered by a vault remain of a tower lying in the NW corner of a bawn about 30m square now reduced to footings, along with the outbuildings in the NE corner and along the south side. There are traces of an outer bawn to the SE. The tower has a spiral stair in the east corner beside a gap facing SE representing the entrance doorway. This castle belonged to Donal O'Hegan in 1574.

Killure Castle

Kilmacduagh Castle

KILLEEN   M348296   C

This tower measuring 6.8m by 6.2m was held in 1574 by William and Redmund McWilliam Burke. The entrance in the north wall was later opened out and another opening also made in the south wall, whilst a recently restored 19th century house adjoins the west side and another building lay to the north. Spiral stairs in the NW corner connect four storeys with vaults over the first and third levels, the latter also having a latrine in the west wall. Some of the upper windows are of two lights.

KILLIMOR   M604284   D

The lower part of a tower measuring 12m by 9m which was held by Dermot O'Daly in 1574 has been incorporated into the west end of a late 18th or early 19th century house of three storeys with a central south doorway. The tower east wall has a blocked ogival-headed doorway and the original entrance doorway recessed within an outer arch with an outer murder-hole between the two. Wooden steps now lie where the spiral stair was in the NW corner. Although inhabited until thirty years ago the building is now derelict.

KILLURE   M800349

Scarps mark out a bawn 40m by 30m around a tower measuring 10.2m by 8.7m with an east-facing entrance. Flanking it is a guard room with a crossloop facing east and a gunloop facing north, and a spiral stair in the SE corner. None of the three surviving main rooms was vaulted but the upper of the two mural chambers over the entrance has traces of a former vault. A passage in the south wall at this level probably led to a latrine.

KILMACDUAGH   R407998   B

Not far north of the ruined cathedral is a palace for the bishop or abbot comprising a block 18.7m long by 8.7m wide over walls 1m thick. The upper level has windows of two lights with seats in the embrasures and was divided into a hall and chamber, although the existing dividing wall is of later date and is not on the original line since it partly obscures one of the windows. The chamber has a latrine in a projection on the north side and has recently been given a new floor and roof. This part of the building was given a third storey and battlements in the later medieval period, when a wing (now reduced to footings) was added in front of the hall entrance at the west end of the south wall.

KILTARTAN or BALLINAMANTAIN   M459047   A

This is a very ruinous 13th century de Burgh castle with a wedge-shaped bailey extending 60m back from a north-facing front wall with a central gatehouse 13m wide with twin round-fronted towers and a portcullis groove in the passage. A keep about 12m square lies in the acute angle at the south end, overlooking a steep drop, the southernmost corner being chamfered off. In the 15th century the basement and storey above of the keep were both subdivided and provided with pointed vaults and a third storey added or rebuilt. The NE wall is thickened to contain the straight main stair. A second narrower stair in the opposite wall is blocked by the flue of a fireplace later inserted in the basement. There are tumbled remains of another tower or building within the bailey NW corner.

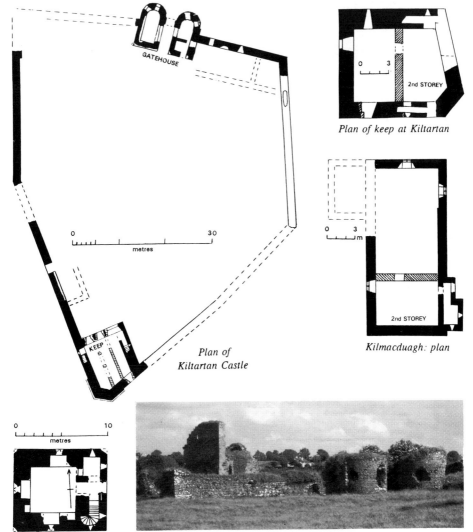

Plan of keep at Kiltartan

Plan of Kiltartan Castle

Kilmacduagh: plan

Killure: plan

Kiltartan Castle

Kiltroge Castle

Lackafinna Castle

KILTROGE   M396330   D

The main body of this tower measuring 10.3m. by 7.2m had four storeys and an attic with in the roof, but the east end wall containing the spiral stair and a tier of rooms over the entrance and guard room rises one level higher. There are corbels for a machicolation over the pointed-headed doorway. The second storey is vaulted and has a fireplace in the north wall. An upper level has a latrine on the south. Some of the loops have ogival heads. The tower lies near the Clare River and in 1574 was held by John Blake.

LACKAFINNA   M629212   D

The second and third storeys of this fragmentary tower measuring just 5.8m by 5.6m have slab-roofed passages on the east side leading to latrines in the SE corner. The third storey main room is vaulted.

LACKAGH   M417365   D

Most of the west corner containing latrines of this tower measuring 11.5m by 9m has been destroyed, and the three levels of passages leading from the spiral stair in the north corner have lost their outer walls. The main body contained three storeys under a vault and a more thinly walled top storey above.

LAVALLYCONNOR   M472162   D

There are now gables on the outer east and west walls of this much-altered tower measuring 10m by 9.3m which has consequently lost its battlements. The east wall contains four levels of rooms over the entrance passage and there is a spiral stair in the SE corner. The main body contained three storeys below a vault and a fourth storey and attic above. The chimney stack on the north side serves a fireplace inserted into a second storey window embrasure. There is a latrine in the west wall.

Lavallyconnor Castle

Lackagh Castle

LEITRIM M686122

This Burke tower measuring about 12m by 10m may be earlier than many of the others since it has a longitudinal crosswall carrying pointed vaults over two cellars with lofts. The NE corner is missing and only fragments remain above the vaults. Any other surviving ancient features are hidden under the vegetation and rubbish.

LISMORE M943161 D

Lismore was an important O'Madden seat, later passing to the Burkes and then to the Dalys of Dunsandle. Three walls 1.5m thick remain standing four storeys high of a tower 12.5m by 9.2m but the thicker east wall containing the staircase and a tier of chambers over the entrance has been destroyed. It faced towards a later extension of which little remains. There is a square bartizan on the SW corner.

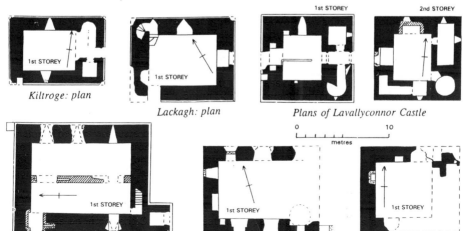
Kiltroge: plan

Lackagh: plan

Plans of Lavallyconnor Castle

Plan of Longford Castle

Plan of Lismore Castle

Killaclogher: plan

LONGFORD   M877120   D

Probably of 13th century origin, but with a later doorway near the NW corner, this building measuring 14.8m by 11.6m has a longitudinal crosswall supporting two vaults high enough to contain both cellars and unlit lofts above. The storey above the vaults was also subdivided and it and a top storey later inserted into the former roof space have fireplaces on the east side and latrines in a turret projecting at the west end of the south wall, which contains a straight staircase. Projecting from the middle of the west side is the south wall with one gunloop of a bawn about 19m wide by 35m long added by the O'Maddens.

LOUGHREA   M622164   B

Loughrea was a major seat of the MacWilliam Uachtair Burkes, later Earls of Clanricarde, the vanished castle to the south by the lough shore having been the caput of Richard de Burgh's mid 13th century lordship in Galway. Low fragments of town walls perhaps of 16th century date remain on the north and west sides of the town and on the east is a gateway now serving as a museum.

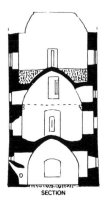

SECTION

LYDACAN   M438080   A

This five storey tower held in the late 16th century by Mautagh O'Heyne was purchased by Galway County Council in 1988. It measures 13m by 10m and rises 16m to a narrow wall-walk now lacking its parapet, although a turret survives over the stair in the SW corner and there is a stump of a roof gable at the east end. On the north side loops in the first and second storeys have been converted into fireplaces. At the level of the first storey vault there is a chamber over the entrance in the west wall, and there are two more such chambers above. Between the uppermost one and the vaulted third storey main room there is a passage from the staircase to a latrine in the north wall. At this level an east-facing window embrasure has access to steps to a room in the southern haunch of the upper vault, above which the walls are much thinner. There is also a fragment of a bawn.

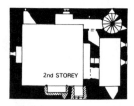

3rd STOREY

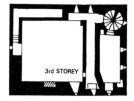

2nd STOREY

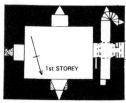

1st STOREY

Town gateway at Loughrea

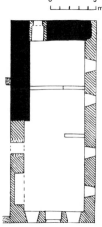

Menlough: plan

Lydacan: plans and section

Doorway at Menlough

Longford Castle

MANNIN   M513168   C

The 5.3m thick east end wall containing the spiral staircase and a tier of large mural chambers over the entrance passage was built in advance of a main tower 9.6m wide which was never added. Adjoining outbuildings of much later date are proof of continued use of the site, but with a decline in status. The SE corner has an angle-loop. The SW corner has recently collapsed.

Mannin: plan

MENLOUGH   M285279   G

On the east bank of the River Corrib south of the village is an early 17th century stronghouse 21.4m long by 9.4m wide with gables in the east side, square bartizans on the NW, NE and SE corners, an entrance at the south end, and a wide fireplace in the lower part of the 1.5m thick west wall. Incorporated at the north end are walls up to 2.2m thick of an older tower about 11m long which in 1574 was held by Thomas Colman. In the 18th century the house was much altered and doubled in width on the west side for most of its length, but it was gutted by fire in 1919 and then left in ruins. See page 50.

Mannin Castle

Lydacan Castle

Menlough Castle

Merlin Castle

MERLIN or DOUGHISKE   M335259

This tower measures 8.9m by 8.2m and has mural chambers in the east wall, whilst the entrance faces north. The main spiral stair lies in the NE corner but there is a service stair in the NW corner down to a vaulted basement kitchen partly below ground. This room has horizontal gunloops and a fireplace. There are other fireplaces in the north wall on the fourth and fifth storeys. There are chambers in the haunches of the vault over the fourth storey. There was a sixth storey in the form of an attic within a gabled roof within a wall-walk with machicolations on the west, south and east sides. The windows all have ogival heads to the lights, including some higher up in pairs. Only an inserted doorway off the staircase, the mark of the roof, and footings remain of a two storey north range perhaps added in the 17th century. Originally known as Doughiske, the castle was held by Stephen Lynch in 1574. The Lynches were forfeited in the 1650s and in 1680 the castle was sold to Francis Blake, whose grandson Francis renamed it Merlin in the mid 18th century.

MONIVEA   M549364   D

This tower was allowed to remain standing when the surrounding later house was demolished c1940. The battlements, doorway and windows are 18th or 19th century except for one two-light window high up on the east side. This building was probably built by the Kellys after a predecessor was destroyed by McWilliam Burke in 1504.

Angle-loop at Merlin

MOYCOLA   M552174   D

Although in plan it looks like a tower, this O'Shaughnessy seat measuring 13.6m by 9.4m was lower in form, with a low living room with small loops and a west end fireplace set over a low cellar. The east end containing the entrance, spiral stair, and mural chambers, is very ruined. A chute on the south side indicates that a third storey once existed.

Moyveela Castle

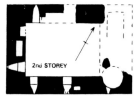

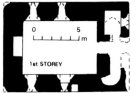

Plans of Moycola Castle

MOYLOUGH   M615490   C

The plinth has been ripped off this hall-house measuring 17.6m by 11.7m over walls 2.5m thick and little remains of the SW end wall. It was built by the de Cotterells, tenants of the de Birminghams, in the 13th century. The lower level has five loops and traces of a possible doorway at the south end of the SE wall. The upper storey had wider lancets and a doorway at the other end of the same wall. From it a spiral stair in the north corner led up to a low third storey which was probably formed later out of the original roof space.

MOYODE   M531231

The second storey of this MacHubert Burkes tower measuring 10.3m by 8.3m has a fireplace, and the third storey has angle-loops to the SE and NW. The entrance and stair lie in the east end wall and there is a latrine at the NW corner. Most of the upper windows each of two ogival-headed lights with a transom were renewed during a recent restoration.

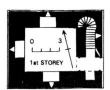

Moyode: plan

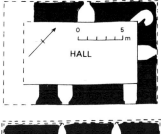

Plans of Moylough Castle

Moylough Castle

MOYVEELA   M448238 D

Only the south wall remains, standing four storeys high with a tier of windows, the uppermost being blocked, and having a wall-walk and parapet on top. There are corbels for a bartizan on the SE corner, whilst the SW corner has evidence of a stair and a join suggesting that this end of the tower was built before the rest of it. See page 51.

NEWTOWN   M423019 D

The O'Shaynes built this large circular 16th century tower house 13.5m in diameter containing rooms 6.5m square positioned so as to allow a rooms over the entrance and guard room on the NE side, with the spiral stair adjoining on the east. Above the lofty vaulted basement there is now just one room with a latrine on the south and ogival-headed loops with fine mouldings and hoodmoulds.

ORANMORE   M377246 C

By the shore is a three storey tower noted in 1574 and 1598 as a possession of the Earl of Clanricarde. It was surrendered to the Confederate Irish in 1643 and to the Parliamentarian Sir Charles Coote in 1651, but was restored to the 6th Earl in 1662. It was then leased to the Blakes until the late 18th century. In 1947 the ruin was sold to Lady Leslie and during the 1960s it was restored for occupation and a low wing added.

The tower measures 15m by 10m and there are subsidiary rooms in a turret 5m square clasping the SE corner, whilst there is a latrine turret 4m wide projecting 1.2m from the east end of the north wall. The entrance lies in the east wall and between it and the SE turret lie stairs in sets of straight flights. The lowest storey has five loops and an inserted fireplace, whilst the second storey is vaulted. On the third storey the eastern mural room has its own latrine in the NE turret, whilst the main hall has a second latrine in the SW corner and stairs rising to upper rooms in both turrets.

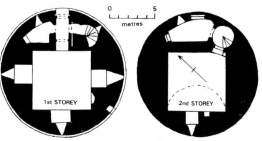

Plans of Newtown Castle

Oranmore Castle

Newtown Castle

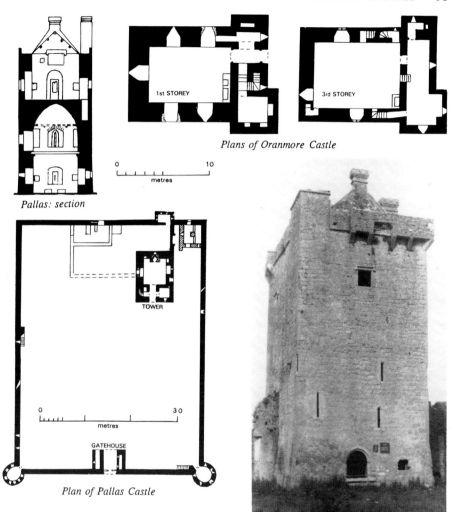

Plans of Oranmore Castle

0   10
metres

Pallas: section

TOWER

0   30
metres

GATEHOUSE

Plan of Pallas Castle

Pallas Castle

PALLAS   M556199   B

The fine tower built by the Burkes in the early 16th century and later held by the Nugents is a roofed but empty national monument. The tower measures 10.8m by 8m and had five storeys with a vault over the third storey loft, the topmost level having a fireplace at one end and being partly in the roof. There are corner loops at second storey level. The lowest storey is lofty enough for the thick end wall containing the spiral staircase to contain within the same hight both the entrance and a mural chamber above, the lowest of a tier of chambers here. The tower lies beside fragments of a later house near one corner of a bawn 52m by 38m with a well-preserved wall 1.1m thick rising 3.9m to where slabs widen the top to allow for both a wall-walk reached by two sets of steps and a parapet with merlons 2.1m high. The bawn has a rectangular flanker behind the tower house and has a show front at the other end with circular corner flankers 4.7m in diameter bristling with gunports and a central gabled gatehouse 7.2m wide projecting 4m within the court and have a box-machicolation over the outer archway.

Pallas Castle

PARK or COOLTYMURRAGHY   M784230 D

In the SW corner of a moated platform 45m square with its ditch best preserved on the north and east sides are remains of the lower parts of the 2.6m thick south and west walls and the SE and NW corners of a 13th century keep about 17m square. It was held by the Kellys in the 16th century. There are traces of four loops. The lost upper storey perhaps had a hall and chamber side-by-side, although no crosswall survives to indicate this.

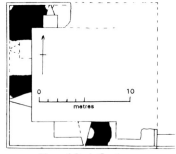

Plan of Park Castle

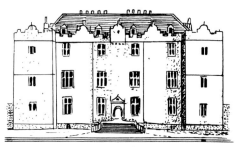

Portumna Castle

Park Castle

PORT ISLAND L533645 A

Known as Cromwell's Barrack, this fort was built in 1656 to command the approach to Bofin Harbour and as a prison for Catholic clergy. It was occupied by Jacobites in 1689-91. The eastern part is a 20m wide regularly-planned fort with an arch entrance through an east range and spearhead shaped corner bastions. The western part, set above a cliff, is more irregularly laid out, with three more bastions and ranges on the north and west.

PORTUMNA M853040 E

This stronghouse with many mullioned windows was built c1618 by Richard Burke, 4th Earl of Clanricarde. He mostly lived in England and rarely used the completed building. The 5th Earl lost Portumna to Henry Cromwell from 1652 until 1661, and the estate was confiscated by William III, but given back by Queen Anne. Until it was gutted by fire in 1826, later earls lived in great state in the house, laying out an elaborate approach from the north with gardens and three outer gates. Minor alterations c1800 included lowering of some of the sills of the basement windows and the addition of a small circular porch in the middle of the south side. The floors and hipped roofs were restored in the 1980s, along with the fine gardens in front of the house. It measures 29.7m by 21.2m over walls up to 1.8m thick and has corner towers 6.5m square containing gunloops. On each storey was a central corridor off which were many rooms with timber dividing walls. The stone walls of the central corridor contain numerous recesses and fireplaces. On the lowest level the southern part contained a low basement kitchen with enormous fireplaces and the northern part has a service doorway on the east side with a drawbar slot. Above are three storeys of fine apartments with a machicolation over the main entrance facing north.

RAHALY M492095

A bawn wall with an added circular NE flanker closely surrounds the north and west walls of a still habitable Burke tower. The western part of the tower only has two full storeys and an attic within the roof and contains an arch bearing the date 1713 with the initials M.D. and N.S. A chamber is built into the haunch of the vault over the upper level and there is a latrine on the south side. The eastern part, which was built first, contains the spiral stair and five upper levels over the entrance passage. The loops are all round-headed except for the several angle-loops.

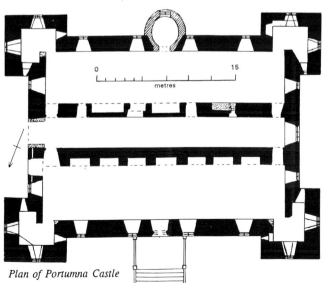

Rahaly Castle   *Plan of Portumna Castle*

Rathgorgin Castle

Trefoil at Roo

RARUDDY   M609188   D

This MacHubert Burke tower measuring 9m by 7.7m has an entrance in the SE wall and cross-loops opening off the spiral stair in the east corner. The lofty second storey is vaulted and has an ogival-headed loop in the SE wall.

RATHGORGIN   M548241   D

Rathgorgin was held by the Dolphins as tenants of the de Burghs and was held by Ullick Burke in 1574. It has fragmentary walls up to 3m high and a ditch around a court measuring 35m by 30m. In the middle of the north side lies the northern half of a building 12.7m by 8.5m with two latrine turrets 3.5m wide projecting at each end of the surviving wall, which has loops on either side of a central fireplace on the second storey. The recess between the turrets was filled in later and was once covered by an arch between them.

RICKS ISLAND   R480992

On an island in Lough Cultra is the overgrown lower part of a tower 11.6m long by 8.5m wide with the SE corner standing to second storey level with a passage all the way through it. A bawn up to 4m wide extends around the south, west and north sides. Its north wall is mostly missing. There is a square turret projecting diagonally from the NW corner of the bawn wall, and a smaller SW corner projection has two latrine chutes. This castle belonged to the Earl of Clanricarde in 1574.

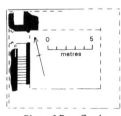

Plan of Roo Castle

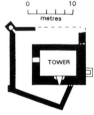

Ricks Island: plan

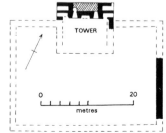

Plan of Rathgorgin Castle

Rinville Castle

Raruddy Castle

Plans of Raruddy Castle

Rinville: plan

Unusual drawbar socket at Roo

RINVILLE   M358225   B

A four storey tower measuring 7.7m by 6.1m with a machicolation in the centre of each side at the top adjoins a modern outbuilding in a park. The stair in the SE corner rises from the entrance on the south side. The second storey has a NE angle-loop and the fourth storey has a two-light window with a transom on the north. Round-headed openings on the west mark the site of a destroyed 18th century wing.

RINVYLE   L657638   C

This tower lay in the NW corner of a bawn and was held in 1574 by Miles MacTibbot. Little remains of the north and east walls. The latter contained chambers over the entrance and a spiral stair in the SE corner. There were three storeys under a vault and at least one more above, where there are the holes of former large windows. One of the upper levels had a latrine in the west wall. Corbels of bartizans remain on the SE and NW corners.

ROO   M516189   D

Only the west wall containing the defaced entrance and a straight stair remains of a tower measuring about 12.4m by 10.4m, although the base of the rest survives under a pile of debris, and there are slight remains of a bawn wall very close to the south side. An embrasure over the entrance has a trefoil-shaped loop. Adjoining it is a latrine reached by a passage in the north wall. There must have been a spiral stair in the SW corner.

ST CLERANS   M555199

An 8m long section of the north wall remains standing up to the fourth storey, where there is a NW corner loop and a window of two cusped-headed lights with a transom and a carved head in the embrasure soffit. This wall also contains a latrine and has evidence of the spiral stair in the NE corner and a vault over the third storey, where there was a corner bartizan. An outbuilding nearby to the south has a window with carved spandrels. The tower belonged to Jonick MacHubert Burke, who was killed whilst in rebellion in 1602. James I granted it to John King of Dublin, but in 1619 it was restored to Moyler MacMoyler Burke. It was forfeited in the 1650s, but restored to the Burkes in 1704. Most of the castle was demolished in the early 19th century by James Hardiman Burke, Sheriff of Galway. His descendants retained the castle when the lands were taken over by the Forestry Commission in 1954.

SEEFIN   M542179   C

The east end wall 8.2m long by 4.3m thick containing the spiral staircase and chambers over the entrance stands five storeys high although it is mostly covered in ivy. Much less remains of the main body added later, making the building about 12m long. It had a vaulted lowest storey. Of the tier of mural rooms only that at third storey level, which has an angle-loop, is vaulted. The castle was held in 1574 by Richard MacUllick Burke.

STRONGFORT or CAHERADANGAN   M526201   C

This restored tower has battlements over the level of the second storey, which has a crossloop in a chamber over the entrance and rooms in circular bartizans on two diagonally opposite corners. It measures 8.9m by 8.2m, two walls being 2m thick at the level of the vaulted lowest storey and the others still thicker, the staircase being in the SE corner. The entrance in the east wall has a thin groove for what must have been an all-metal portcullis.

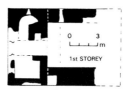

Seefin: plan

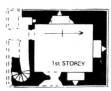

Tawnamore: plan

Strongfort Castle

Tawnamore Castle

Doorway at Strongfort

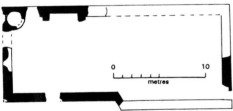

Plan of Terryland Castle

Seefin Castle

TAWNAGHMORE   M412425   D

The outer part of the south wall end containing a tier of two vaulted chambers over the entrance and the spiral stair in the SE corner has fallen. In the same height the main body contains just a basement and a lofty vaulted upper room with a fireplace in the NE corner. When complete the tower measured 11.8m by 8.2m and in 1574 was held by Moyler MacRichard. It lay in the NW corner of a bawn platform.

TERRYLAND   M294264   C

Near a new bridge over the River Corrib are fragmentary remains of a early 17th century house built by the Earl of Clanricarde on the site of a tower held in 1574 by Dominick Lynch. Of three storeys and an attic, the house measured 25m by 10m wide at the best preserved north end where there is an oven and kitchen fireplace in the east wall at ground level. The north gable has a row of chimneystacks set diagonally and corbels for a square bartizan. Two-light windows with hoodmoulds remain in the west wall. The south end, now just footings, was wider, suggesting two periods of work. The house lay in the SE corner of a bawn about 42m square, of which the east and north walls partly remain.

TUAM   M435520   C

Adjoining the south boundary wall of a supermarket carpark is the lower part of a south-facing D-shaped bawn flanker 3m in diameter. It probably formed part of the castle held in 1574 by the archbishop of Tuam, although it lies some distance from Shop Street, where the castle is said to have been located. Roderick O'Connor erected a "castrum mirificum" at Tuam in 1161.

TULLIRA   M474097

In 1882 Edward Martin built a new house alongside and inserted large windows into the lowest two levels of a five storey tower house with a vault over the fourth storey. The Martins had obtained what was originally a Burke tower by 1598. The tower has a machicolation over the entrance and original two-light windows on the third and fourth storeys. Some of the loops have ogival heads and there is a latrine in the NW corner.

TULLOKYNE   M237368   C

The west side 10.8m long stands five storeys high on a rock with evidence of mural rooms at the north end up as far as the fourth storey vault. Also known as Caislean na gCailleach, this tower was held in 1574 by Murtagh O'Connor. Nothing remains of a second tower nearby which collapsed in 1839.

WITCHES   M468348

The south end is now missing of a small 13th century hall-house 7.4m wide over walls up to 1.5m thick, probably once about 11m long. The only features are slit windows, only one having a wide embrasure, plus a doorway at the north end of the west wall to a former corbelled-out latrine. This castle was held by Murragh McSwiney in 1574.

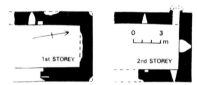

Plans of Witches Castle

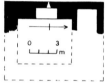

Tullokyne: plan

Strongfort: plan

Tullira Castle

Tullokyne Castle

Witches Castle

OTHER CASTLE REMAINS IN COUNTY GALWAY

ARD L751312 Fragments of east and north walls of tower 10m by 15.8m up to 5m high. Held by "Tege na Buly" O'Flaherty in 1574

ARDRUMKILLA M350509 Low drystone wall 1.6m thick around bawn 40m by 32m with gateway on SE with footings of adjoining building. Traces of tower in north corner.

AUGHRIM M790284 Platform 35m by 25m with walling remaining on either side of possible gateway 3.5m wide. Probably early site, held by Callogh O'Kelly in 1574.

BALLINDONAGH M082572 11m high fragment of Lynch tower with east facing entrance and stair between two storeys above level of damaged vault.

BALLYDAVID M511303 Footings of tower 11m by 9m with fragment of wall 1m thick.

BALLYDOOGAN M679169 Thin walls in garden wall. Ogival window-head loose on site.

BALLYGASTY M621185 Shapeless fragments upon a mound of debris.

BALLYMURPHY M391307 Just a fragment of the south wall now remains.

BIRMINGHAM M468530 Platform 48m by 40m and up to 4m high with footings of bawn wall and several buildings. Building outside south corner has traces of fallen vault.

BUNOWEN L603421 Fragments of bawn wall 2m high. Mound on site of tower. An O'Flaherty castle.

CAHERMORRIS M342424 Low fragments and debris of possible gateway of castle held by Burke of Castle Hacket in 1570. Listed as held by the MacWalters sept in 1574.

CAISLEAN BEG M571653 Mound of debris and low fragments of tower 7.3m square.

CALLOW M720342 16m long wall with one loop to west of farmhouse is relic of castle held by William O'Kelly in 1574.

CARNAUN M478313 Turret, other fragments and footings within ringwork 55m by 30m.

CARNMORE M411284 Low ivy-covered building 11m wide by up to 7.4m wide over walls 1m thick with traces of bawn wall to west.

CASTLE CON M493035 Traces of bawn 48m by 38m surround 2m thick SE wall of O'Shaughnessy tower 10m long with signs of vault, stairwell and latrine-shaft. p63.

CASTLE ELLEN M491320 Four storey high west end of tower containing fireplaces (but possibly a later folly). Adjoining thick section of bawn wall with gateway. See p38.

CASTLE FREEKY M365484 Remains of drystone building within 45m diameter ringfort.

CLADDAGH M532552 Footings and low NW corner of O'Kelly tower 12m by 8m. Shown by Grose as four storeys high with machicolation over central pointed-arched entrance.

CLARETUAM M400496 2m high and 1.3m fragment of wall incorporated in field wall. Site of castle held in 1574 by Redmund MacMoyler MacRic.

CLOGHANOWER M276451 1.8m thick SW wall of tower 8.3m wide with bartizan on south corner at second storey, and passage within wall at third storey level. See p63.

CLOONCURREEN M569399 Base and fallen fragments of tower 10m by 7m held in 1574 by Dermot O'Mannin.

CLOONEEN M745055 Small vaulted room in projection beyond surviving corner of thinly walled main tower with interior choked with vegetation.

CLOONORAN M626463 9m long wall fragment of building also called Castle Bellew.

DOON L614538 Fragments of bawn on west and north edges of rock. Later building has tall gable. Held by Edmund O'Flaherty in 1574.

DOONBALLY M457597 Fragments of tower on summit 15m by 10m of motte within egg-shaped bailey 40m by 28m with ditch. Held by Thomas Balve in 1574.

DROUGHT M677193 Defaced and featureless lower part of southern end of possible hall-house 11m wide. Later turret added to south end of west wall.

DRUMGRIFFIN M347374 5m high fragment of a tower held in 1574 by Ullick Row.

EYRECOURT M919168 Slight remains of O'Madden tower converted into dovecot by Eyres. 1926 photo shows arch from it to vanished 17th century block with north wing.

FIDDAUN M636538 Rubble pile on site of a tower held in 1574 by Malaghlin MacAnabe.

GALLAGH M684428 Mound 8m high with traces of wall around 15m diameter summit. Destroyed in 1504 by MacWilliam Burke. House beside it with six chimneys has gone.

GARRAFINE M692403 2m high fragment of tower. Rest collapsed in gale in 1980s.

GALBOLEY M624229 Two 3m high fragments of building 5.8m wide on moated platform. Held in 1574 by Olyverus Burke.

GORTNAMACKAN M573148 Fragment of north corner with part of stair of tower held in 1574 by Ullick Caragh MacEdmund.

HEADFORD M271470 5.5m square bawn flanker with later brick vaults nay be relic of castle of Aghkyne held 1574 by Redmund MacWalter. Possible site of Walter de Riddlesford's castle of 1230s.

INISHMOR L810122 Rubble-filled 1m high base of massive O'Brien tower 10m by 9m.

INISHROO M326106 5m high debris mound on coastal promontory. Wall at east end of ditch at south end. An O'Heyne tower destroyed by the earthquake of 1755.

KILCOOLY M692164 Fragment of wall and mound of debris of Burke tower. Old drawing shows farmhouse with one tower west of it and another to the north.

KILCORNAN M425209 Redington family house (mental institute) incorporates altered tower held by Redmund Burke in 1598. His son was executed by Cromwell in 1650.

KILLACLOGHER M548380 NW corner of tower 11m by 9m three storeys high with traces of vault. Held in 1574 by Donell O'Kelly. Later armorial plaque on west wall.

KILLEEN M808313 Mound of debris of O'Kelly castle destroyed to build nearby railway.

KILMACRAH M673136 Featureless 3m high thin walls of NW corner of tower. Pile of stone beyond road to SE.

KILTULLAGH M618593 Debris and base of tower held 1574 by Hubert O'Conchanon.

KNOCKANARRA M622718 Recently destroyed 13.4m long north wall and stubs of adjoining walls of tower on west bank of Island River held in 1574 by Cloghane Kellibig.

LERHIN M583580 Debris pile of Burke tower partly standing two storeys high in 1969 lies in east corner of 40m square bawn with NE wall 2.5m high. Second bawn to SE.

LETTERMULLAN L850225 3m high defaced fragment. Held by Morogh MacHugh in 1584.

LISCANANAUN M357357 Debris of west wall which collapsed c1990. Had evidence of fireplaces and vault over third of four storeys. Held in 1574 by Tibbot Leigh.

MACE M312392 NE half of tower stands three storeys high. The surviving end wall contains the entrance, stairwell and a room. One SE loop has a gunloop below it.

MINNA M016208 Footings 9m by 7.3 of west and south walls by shore. Scene of Walter Fada Burke's murder in 1549 by Donnell Fitz-Rory O'Flaherty.

MOYCULLEN M233331 Bawn wall 5m high and 1.6m thick around orchard 35m across marks site of castle held in 1574 by Rory O'Flaherty.

NEWCASTLE M293260 Small castle, bawn and thatched cabin mentioned in 1657. A circular bawn flanker lies close to River Corrib in University grounds.

PARKANASSA or CLOGHAILL M370270 Deeply ditched platform 115m by 65m. Arch once visible has now gone.

PARK WEST M594588 Low fragment of tower NE corner on platform 16m by 10m with traces of possible bawn wall extending 15m to the north of it.

SHANCLOGH M435249 4m high fragment of south wall of small tower with traces of vault hidden away in thicket. See plan on page 63.

TIAQUIN M568352 Platform 24m by 10m with pieces of rubble marks site of tower held in 1574 by Malaghlin O'Kelly.

TOBERBRACKAN M442210 Just a 1.5m high fragment of the south wall. Reported former tablet dated 1643 with initials of John Lynch and his wife Mary.

TOOLOOBAUNBEG M592214 1m thick south wall remains of tower 8m wide and about 12m long with archway in middle. SW part survives of bawn 65m square.

WALLSCOURT M688204 Vaulted lowest level of a tower lies near fragment of two storey house of Blake family with chimney stacks on end wall and along one side.

Reduced to mounds of rubble: BALLINDRIMNA M722138, BALLYCOONEY M586132, KILLINNY M392056, LISSANARD M783094, OCHIL BEG M878222, TOLENDAL M445581. The tower on an island at M799020 in Lough Derg is probably 19th century.

Buried footings remain of a building of uncertain purpose at Streamstown M718130.

Castle Conn: plan

Town Gate, Athenry

Kinvarra: plan

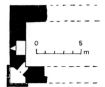

Clochanawer: plan

SITES OF CASTLES IN GALWAY

BALLAGH M820252 Part of wall in D-shaped enclosure 20m across with earth bank.

BALLINA M489444 Traces of bawn 40m by 25m. Held by Richard Burke in 1574.

BALLYBANAGHER Tower held by Thomas Ballagh in 1574 lay near confluence of Grange and Clare rivers.

BALLYGAR M776525 Site of castle of "Beallagharee" held in 1574 by Hugh MacTirilagh.

BALLYGLASS M664700 Site of castle said to have been occupied by Nuala na Meadoige.

BARNA M248236 Site by stream of tower held in 1574 by Owen O'Halloran.

BLACK CASTLE M854037 Vanished tower on shore near Portumna. Garrisoned in 1659.

BROOK LODGE Site of Cahirnefieke castle held in 1574 by Tirlagh Carragh MacSwyne.

CAHERNALEE M567238 Slight traces of tower and surrounding bawn 30m by 22m.

CARNONEEN M407358 Last low featureless wall 1.5m thick of tower held in 1574 by Thomas Balve was destroyed c1970. It stood very close to the Catholic church.

CARROWBROWNE M317301 Tower held in 1574 by Donell Oge O'Halloghan stood 16m high until its collapse and replacement by a late 19th century house, now itself a ruin.

CASHLAUNATREENODE M624658 Small enclosure on site of MacKegan castle.

CASTLEBOY M524108 Last remains of hall house with four surviving loops and latrine shoot quarried away for gravel in 1982. Held by Redmond MacHubert Roe in 1574.

CASTLE MOELL M497505 Dressed stones in field walls are the only relics of Edmund MacMelaghin's tower.

CASTLE TOGHER M646688 Site of castle held in 1574 by the sons of Tibbot Ullick.

CLOONIGNY M764339 Platform 65m square with ramparts and ditch marks site of castle held in 1574 by Shane Nemoy.

CLOONLEE M717108 Site of Castle de Burgh.

CREAGH M862328 Large semi-circular platform on site of O'Kelly castle.

DOON M734361 Site of castle held in 1574 by Teige MacMelaghlin O'Kelly.

FOUGH M124432 Site of O'Flaherty tower on natural bridge over Owenriff River.

GARBALLY M832303 Ornamental spire on site of tower held in 1574 by Maher MacTully.

GORT M453022 Fragments of barracks on site of O'Shaughnessy bawn and tower stormed by Ludlow in June 1651, the garrison leaders being put to the sword.

KILCOLGAN M412180 Early 19th century house on site of tower of Clanricarde Burkes. Soldiers from Galway scaled bawn wall in 1665 and drove off the servants.

LARAGH M585286 Site of castle held in 1574 by Shane O'Daly.

LISNASHEIL M794226 D-shaped platform 53m across is site of an O'Donellan castle.

LYDACAN M377312 House demolished in 1992 included old wall with spiral staircase.

MOANBAWN M475289 Overgrown pentagonal platform 40m by 26m.

MULLAGHMORE M585459 Site of castle held in 1574 by Teige McWilliam O'Kelly.

NEWCASTLE M545326 Site of tower held in 1574 by Connor O'Kelly quarried away.

OGHERY M192364 Footings of later house on site of tower on small island in Ross Lake held by Jonick O'Halloran in 1574.

ROSCAM M351248 19th century quay on site of tower held in 1574 by Walter Burke.

SHANBALLY M485199 Slight rise in field represents former bawn.

OTHER CASTLE SITES: Annaghbride M686153, Ballingarry M581142, Ballintemple M619128, Castlebin M680283, Castlefield M623741, Castle French M489382, Castlegar M438186, Castle Rodger M794355, Cloonbrusk M548296, Levally M544525, Lisamoltaun M698287, Mackney M827291, Menlough M620415, Moneyduff M383234. Uncertain sites: Benmore M641220, Boleynanollag M790852.

GAZETTEER OF CASTLES IN COUNTY LEITRIM

CASTLE JOHN   H033084

This thinly walled house by Lough Scur is named after Sean MacRannall, a noted tyrant who sided with the English and who was known as "John of the Heads" because of the large numbers of people he had decapitated. It measures 17m by 8m and has tiers of fireplaces at each end and a semi-circular stair turret in the middle of the north side, and the entrance opposite it on the south. A small ivy-clad tower containing rooms 3m square on an island in the nearby lough is thought to have been a prison.

CASTLETOWN or GARR   G838413   D

The western end of a 16th century tower 9.4m wide and once 14m long set on a rock by a stream has a ground level kitchen fireplace flanked by loops. One jamb remains of a fireplace in the north wall at second storey level.

DROMAHAIR   G804310   D

All that remains of the chief seat of the O'Rourkes captured in 1588 by a surprise attack by the Earl of Clanricarde and Sir Richard Bingham is a ruined and overgrown block containing a hall 22m long by 7.5m wide within ivy-covered walls 1.3m thick set on a rock near the River Bonet. Several window embrasures remain, plus two doorways in the more complete northern side. Nearby to the east is a much-altered stronghouse built in 1626 by Sir Edward Villiers to replace the original tower house. The south wall of the main block 21m long by 10.6m wide is very ruined. The north wall was thickened to contain latrines, the fine fireplaces (one at ground level has an oven) and the well of a former spiral staircase, and has two wings each 6.8m wide projecting 5.6m beyond it. See page 67.

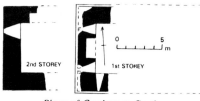

Plans of Castletown Castle

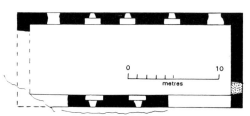

Plan of hall at Dromahair

Castletown Castle

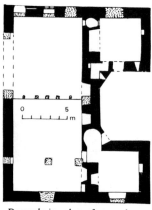

Dromahair: plan of stronghouse

LOUGH RINN   M099935

At the SW corner this round-cornered tower still stands 7m high. The walls are 1.2m thick and there is a vault over the basement. There are remains of a stair to the east of a doorway on the south side and a double-splayed loop facing east. It belonged to the MacRannalls, who anglicised their name to Reynolds c1580.

MANORHAMILTON   G884398   C

This impressive stronghouse built in 1638 by Sir Frederick Hamilton was only occupied until 1652, when it was wrecked by the forces of the 5th Earl of Clanricarde It has two wings 9m wide which projected 8m beyond the destroyed north wall of a four storey main block 10m wide by 24.5m long. Many extra bedrooms were provided in four corner towers roughly 5.5m square but with acute outermost angles so that the outer faces could be fully flanked. The west wing has remains of a large kitchen fireplace at ground level. A bawn with its own flankers at each corner except the NW closely surrounds the house on the west, north and east, and opens into a court on the south side. The church to the SE lies in the middle of a walled graveyard with spearhead-shaped flankers. See page 67.

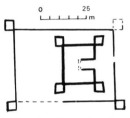

Manorhamilton: site plan

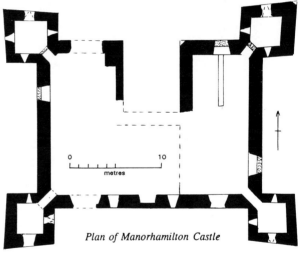

Plan of Manorhamilton Castle

Stronghouse at Dromahair   *Manorhamilton Castle*

Parke's Castle

PARKE'S   G783351   E

Francisco de Cuellar, a survivor from an Armada ship, was sheltered here by Sir Brian O'Rourke in 1588. De Cuellar describes his host as permanently at war with the Protestant English. Excavations in 1974 revealed the base of a 16th century tower 9.5m by about 17m long which is assumed to have been destroyed by the English authorities after O'Rourke was hanged in London in 1591. It seems to have had thick walls containing extra chambers at each end, one of these tiers of chambers having been built before the rest of the tower. Around it is a pentagonal bawn with the 33m long south side rising direct from the waters of Lough Gill. A round tower 5.7m in diameter lies at the most vulnerable northern corner, and there is a round turret later remodelled as a dovecote at the NW corner, whilst the SE corner has a 17th century pepperpot-roofed turret. There was once a dry moat around the landward sides. In the 1620s the castle was transferred to Captain Robert Parke, who built a three storey house with numerous upper mullioned windows on the east side, incorporating the round tower and adjoining a new gatehouse with narrow guardrooms set on either side of the passageway. These parts were re-roofed in the 1980s. The castle, then known as Newtown, was captured for the Confederate Catholics by the O'Harts, and in 1652 was surrendered to the Cromwellian Sir Charles Coote. The last occupant was Robert Gore, son of Robert Parke's daughter Anne.

ROSSCLOGHER   G884398   D

On an islet at the south side of Lough Melvin are remains of the chief seat of the MacClanceys comprising a roughcasted round tower surrounded by a thick breastwork with a loopholed bastion facing the nearby shore. The Armada survivor Francesco de Cuellar (see Parke's Castle) defended the castle against the English Lord Deputy, Sir William FitzWilliam in 1588.

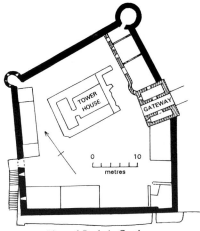

Plan of Parke's Castle

Manorhamilton Castle

Fireplace at Dromahair

Rossclogher Castle

OTHER CASTLES IN COUNTY LEITRIM

CHERRY ISLAND H197112 Very ruined stronghouse by Garidice Lough measures 19.5m
   by 8m over walls 1.2m thick up to 2.5m high at north end with stony bank enclosing
   bawn to north, east and south.
CORAGELY H072093 Vault arch 2m high supported on walls 1.5m thick alone remains.
DUNCARBURY G788576 Small bawn with footings of walls on east and west, a pile of
   rubble on north, and a wall 7m long, 2m high and 1m thick on south side. Probably a
   Clancy stronghold.
JAMESTOWN Gateway alone survives of town wall built in 1622 by Sir Charles Coote.
SRADOON G782319 4.5m high curved turret of castle built by the Harrisons on an island
   in Bonet River.

CASTLE SITES IN COUNTY LEITRIM

Aughry (stronghouse) N049896, Belhavel G867294, Cloncorick H237042, Corry
G958271, Kilmore G785348, Longfield H243072, Port G953034

GAZETTEER OF CASTLES IN COUNTY MAYO

AGHALAHARD   M140570 A

This castle was the chief seat of a branch of the MacDonnells, who were originally mercenaries serving the Burkes. It was captured in 1596 by the Earl of Clanricarde in collaboration with the English commanders D'Arcy and Brabazon. Much survives of the 1.5m thick wall of the irregularly hexagonal bawn about 30m across set on a rock platform with a large building in the SE corner and a show front on the NW, where the wall is thicker, contained a gateway, and was flanked at either end by square turrets, although that at the south end is now very ruined. In the SW corner lies the western half of a tower house measuring 11.8m by 8.6m formerly with a spiral stair in the NE corner, next to the east-facing entrance. Above the vaulted third storey was a more thinly walled fourth storey of which only the north side now remains. There was a second bawn to the south.

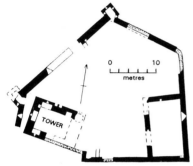

Plan of Aghalahard Castle

BALLINGLEN   G103350 D

The north wall of this 14th century tower measuring 12.4m by 10m has partly collapsed, but a straight stair leading up from the basement survives, its loop being blocked by a thickening of this wall in a later rebuilding which also saw the addition of a projection at the north end of the east wall. The second storey has a latrine in the SE corner and remains of a high vault with a chamber in the southern haunch. The third storey has a fireplace, and a mullion-and-transom window hidden under ivy.

Ballinglen: view showing added outer face of north wall

Aghalahard Castle

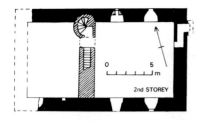

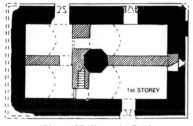

Plans of Ballycurrin Castle

Ballisnahyny Castle

BALLISNAHYNY   M234517   D

This 13th century hall-house measuring 13m by 9.8m has traces of what may be an original vault over the upper storey, a unique feature for such a building. Three upper window embrasures survive, along with jambs of two others ruined by the loss of the south corner. There is also a doorway leading out to a former latrine at the north end of the NW wall. Three loops and the jamb of a fourth remain in the lower level.

BALLYCURRIN   M194492   D

The upper part of the west wall has been destroyed of this 13th century hall house measuring 19.8m by 12m at the base of the steeply battered walls. A large central octagonal pier to carry the floor beams of the hall and chamber set end-to-end was later incorporated into crosswalls dividing the lower storey into four cellars with pointed vaults. The wall across the width of the building is thick enough to contain a straight stair connecting the two levels, but had to be still further thickened at the north end to contain a spiral stair leading to a third storey then created over the private chamber at the west end. The hall itself remains fairly intact, with two window embrasures on each of the north and south sides and a passage to a latrine in a slight projection from the east end wall. Ballycurrin was held by Ullick MacSeoinin Burke in 1574. It was acquired by the Earl of Clanricarde in 1610 and was leased to Maurice Lynch in 1679, his descendants inhabiting a nearby house until the death of Charles Lynch in 1894. See photo on page 9.

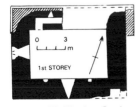

Plan of Ballinglen Castle

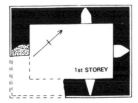

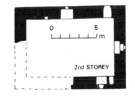

Plans of Ballisnahyny Castle

Ballylahan Castle

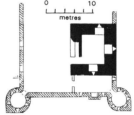

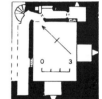

Ballyhowly Castle

Plans of Ballyhowly Castle

BALLYHOWLY   M379815   D

A 15th century tower measuring 11m by 9.8m lies in the middle of the SE side of a 16th century bawn which has lost its NE end but which retains circular two storey flankers 5.2m in diameter at the west and south corners. These flankers had fireplaces backed against triangular prows filling the dead outermost ground that could not be covered by fire from the next flanker. The tower has a damaged entrance and straight staircase in the NW wall, and just a couple of steps remain of a spiral stair leading up from the second storey in the northern corner. The outer wall and vault of the straight stair have fallen, leaving just the thin inner wall to precariously carry the vault over the very lofty second storey main room. At this second level a passage in the NE end wall leads past a latrine to a small chamber in the east corner. A chamber in the SW end wall at vault level must have been reached down from the main room over the vault (now inaccessible), which has one fine two-light window facing SE. The castle belonged to the MacMorris family.

BALLYKINE   M114570   A

In the later medieval period, when the castle was held by the gallowglas MacDonnells, a wing about 4m square above its battered base was added to the south end wall of a two storey 13th or 14th century building measuring 9m by 7.4m over walls 1m thick, the northern part of which seems to have contained a gateway passage through to an earlier enclosure. The passage was blocked up and the west side was given a narrow extension containing a stair rising up an upper doorway set over a passage to a lower doorway, whilst the east side was given a three buttresses supporting arches carrying a wall-walk. What look like machicolation slots are actually openings resulting from the buttresses having cracked away from the older building. The wing contains four storeys with the third one vaulted. The castle is hidden in dense woodland, barely visible from a nearby track.

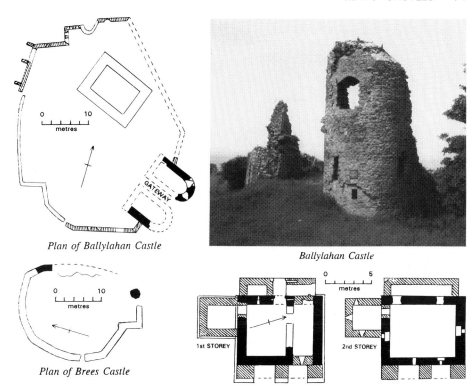

Plan of Ballylahan Castle

Ballylahan Castle

Plan of Brees Castle

1st STOREY   2nd STOREY

Plans of Ballykine Castle

BALLYLAHAN   M274989 A

The fragmentary remains of a gatehouse 15m wide with two U-shaped towers flanking a central passage lie on the east side of a polygonal court about 40m by 34m containing footings of a hall-keep measuring about 14m by 11m. Little now remains of the southern tower of the gatehouse, although the structure is depicted in a more complete state in an engraving of the 1790s. There were buildings on the west side of the court, which is of irregular outline with work of several periods, including walling with 16th century gunloops and arches supported on piers. The castle is thought to have been founded by Jordan d' Exeter in the mid 13th century, his descendants being known as the MacJordans.

BREES   M298810 D

On a commanding height are defaced and tumbled remains of the battered lower parts of a polygonal curtain wall up to 1.6m thick around a court about 21m by 18m with a tower measuring about 8m by 6m, perhaps a gatehouse, or maybe a later tower house, projecting 3m beyond the south end. The castle belonged to the MacMorris family.

BURRISHOOLE   L963954 & L966955 A

By a private house on a coastal headland is a fragment of a long south wall with a blocked arch with a second length of ancient walling nearby. The south transept west wall and the cloister north wall of the Dominican friary founded in 1486 by Richard Burke on the opposite side of the estuary have gunloops dating from 1580 when Sir Nicholas Malbie converted the building into an English garrison post against the neighbouring O'Malleys.

Carn Castle

Castle Burke

CARN or CORRAUN   M234951 & M235952

West of Bellavary (where there was originally another tower) are remains of a 13th or 14th century chamfered-cornered building about 16.5m long by 11.4m wide over walls up to 2.8m thick, the northern part standing three storeys high with a passage high up on the east side, where there are remains of two window embrasures at second storey level. Only slight traces remain of what appears to have been a straight staircase rising from south to north through the length of the west wall facing the Toormore River. On a low hillock, perhaps a motte, just 50m away to the NE are tumbled fragments of a second massive building. Jordan d' Exeter's descendants the MacStephens held this estate in 1617.

CARRICKKILDAVNET   M720941   B

There are machicolations in the middle of each of the north, south and west sides of this O'Malley tower on Achill Island, which measures just 6.9m by 5.6m over walls 1.7m thick and has a vaulted cellar and a stair in the west wall. Just 1.6m away from the west and north sides is the lower part of a bawn wall 0.8m thick with a circular SW flanker.

CASTLEAFFY   L950884   C

Close to the shore the NE half still stands three storeys high of a tower 9.7m wide over walls 2.2m thick which appears to have been 12m long. The surviving stub of the NW wall contains the entrance doorway with a straight stair rising from it, and a chamber above with a murder hole in its floor. Above is a passage in the haunch of the vault over the second storey, at which level there is a latrine in the east corner.

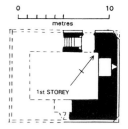

Plan of Castleaffy

CASTLE BURKE or KINVOYNELL   M166773   C

Lying in a farmyard is a five storey tower measuring 12.5m by 9.6m with narrow mural chambers over the entrance in the south side-wall and latrine passages in the west end wall with a spiral stair in the SW corner. There are gunloops and angleloops and the fourth storey is a dark loft tucked under a vault below the main hall. The SE corner of the building collapsed a few years ago. Originally called Kinvoynell, the castle was renamed Castle Burke after being granted to Mikes Burke, 4th Viscount Mayo. His successor sold the castle to the Brownes of Westport.

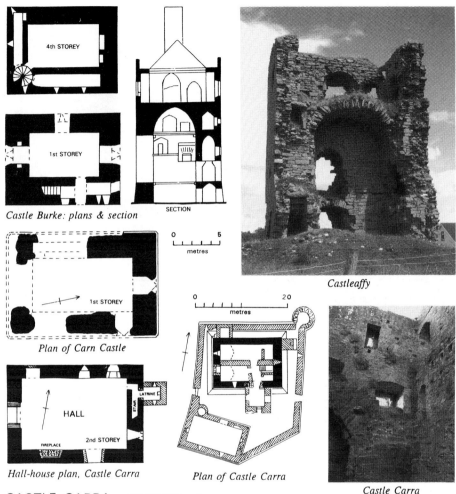

Castle Burke: plans & section

SECTION

Castleaffy

Plan of Carn Castle

Hall-house plan, Castle Carra

Plan of Castle Carra

Castle Carra

CASTLE CARRA   M172753   A

Above Lough Carra is a hall-house 15m long by 10.5m wide built by the de Stauntons in the early 13th century. It had an upper entrance facing north. The lower entrance facing south may not be original but existed by the 14th century when a porch was added in front of it and a turret containing a latrine opening off the staircase to the wall-walk was added on the east, and a second turret built in front of the upper entrance. The MacEvilly descendants of the de Stauntons inserted a longitudinal crosswall and vaults in the lower storey, added a battered plinth, and surrounded the building with a small polygonal bawn with a large outbuilding in the SW corner and gateways facing east and west. After it was surrendered to the Crown in the 1570s the castle was granted to Captain William Bowen and he strengthened the bawn by adding a circular flanker 4.5m in diameter with numerous gunloops on the vulnerable NE corner. About 50m further out on this side the promontory was cut off by a wall flanked by gunloops in the side walls of a square outer gatehouse. In the 1660s the castle passed to Sir Henry Lynch, whose descendants held it until the 19th century.

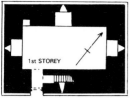

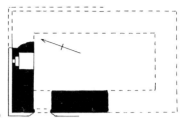

Plan of Cloonnagashel Castle

Plan of Castle Connor

CASTLE CONNOR   G258242 D

Peter de Birmingham is thought to have founded this castle on a low promontory by the River Moy in the 1230s. Of a hall-house 10.6m wide and possibly 18n long part of the west wall remains with a doorway and a section of the north wall with one voussoired window embrasure. The castle was later taken over by the Burkes but in 1371 was captured by the O'Connors and perhaps destroyed. The traces of a bawn facing the approach and a fragment of a gatehouse may date from when the O'Dowds rebuilt the castle in 1520. Tadhg O'Dowd fell from the battlements to his death in 1580, and in 1594 his son David (then holding the castle under O'Connor Sligo overlordship as a result of a grant of 1584) was murdered here at his own fireside by an English soldier. The O'Dowds were dispossessed in 1656, their lands here going to Lewis Wingfield.

CASTLE KNOCK or CAISLEAN NA COILLE   M175565 B

Completely hidden in a thicket is the lowest storey with three loops of a tower measuring 9.8m by 8m. There is a latrine-chute on the north side. The east wall contains a spiral stair in the NE corner and the rebuilt entrance doorway with a small room in the SE corner.

CASTLE MAGARRET   M347710 C

This 13th century hall house of the FitzGeralds, later Earls of Kildare, beside the Robe River measures 16m by 13.6m over walls 2.6m thick above a battered base. The north and south corners are chamfered, although the west corner close to a projection containing a latrine on the NW side is square, whilst the east corner and most of the adjoining walls have been destroyed. The latrine served a private room with its own fireplace in the SW end wall divided off by a partition from the main hall occupying the rest of that level. The basement has three loops in the NW wall and was also probably divided by timber partitions, but no evidence of them or any later vaults or dividing walls survive. Two similarly divided upper storeys were later created within the upper part of the hall and chamber and the roof-space above them, perhaps in the period when Sir Richard Bingham occupied the castle, following its recovery after capture in 1548 by O'Connor Don and the MacDermots. It was later held by the Browne family, but from 1694 until 1966 they lived in a new house on the other side of the road to the north.

Castle Connor

Cloonnagashel Castle

Castle Magarret

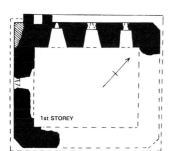

Clare Island Castle

Plans of Castle Magarret

Castle Knock: plan

CLARE ISLAND   M715851   B

This ruined three storey O'Malley tower associated with Grace O'Malley beside the harbour has square bartizans containing rooms opening off the second of three unvaulted storeys. The exterior is cemented and alterations were made in 1831 to convert it into a coastguard station.

CLOONNAGASHEL   M230670   D

Maurice Fitz-Gerald is thought to have had a castle here in the 1230s. Although it has a slightly more elongated plan than most tower houses, being 14m long by 9.7m wide, the features of the existing building appear to be entirely 15th century. The SE wall contains a long straight stair rising from an entrance with a portcullis slot to where a spiral stair begins in the east corner at second storey level. The main room at this level has four embrasures, one with access to a latrine in the north corner. Another, containing the portcullis winding gear, has access to a chamber occupying the whole length of the SW wall, an arch being provided internally to widen the wall to contain this chamber. The mass grave of fifteen female Burkes hanged here by their arch-enemy Sir Richard Bingham, Governor of Connacht from 1558 onwards, is said to be alongside the castle.

CREEVAGH   M202609

Only the base buried in a pile of debris remains of a tower about 8m by 7m lying in the NE corner of a bawn about 20m square enclosed by a fragmentary wall 1.1m thick with remains of an outbuilding on the west side. The south side lies upon a low cliff and there is a projecting turret 3.7m wide set on a rock at the SE corner. Only footings of the wall and traces of an outbulding remain of a pentagonal outer bawn.

CREGDUFF   M254582

The lofty vaulted basement with three loops remains of a tower measuring 10.5m by 8.6m. The very ruined east wall contained a spiral stair in the NE corner and a zig-zag entrance passage with the outer doorway covered by a loop from the main room. The next storey also mostly survives intact but its features are obscured by vegetation. One of the upper levels had a latrine in the west wall.

DEEL or CASTLE GORE   G180184

There is a square bartizan on the NW corner of the wall-walk of this tower measuring 12.2m by 10.2m which must be 16th century since there are gunloops opening off the spiral stair in the NE corner and the only vaults are those of the mural rooms over the entrance in the north wall. Remodelling in the 18th and 19th centuries has obscured the upper fireplaces in the west and south walls and the assumed latrines in the SE corner. A much less massive 17th century wing to the south has also been much altered but it retains a bartizan containing a small room at the third storey SW corner and evidence of fireplaces at the south end. The building seems to have remained in use until the 1920s.

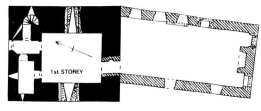

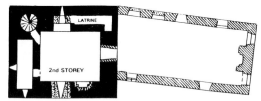

Plans of Deel Castle

Deel Castle   *Doonamona: plan*   *Cregduff: plan*

Creevagh Castle

Doonamona Castle

DOOCASTLE   G583086

Hidden under ivy (which obscures the upper features) and set within a cluster of trees lie three walls of a building 11m wide over walls 2m thick which was at least 15m long, probably a 13th century hall house. There is a long straight stair in the north wall. A later longitudinal crosswall in the lowest level has been entirely removed but the scars remain of the vaults it once supported. A doorway on the south side at ground level faces towards a bawn 7m wide and 12m long enclosed by a wall 1.2m thick. See page 4.

DOONAMONA   M204812   C

The NE wall stands high of a tower measuring 10.8m by 9.2m, together with part of the NW wall. Part of the stairwell remains in the east corner with a passage from it to a latrine at second storey level, where the north corner has a broken angle-loop.

DUNCARTON   F798382

This promontory fort contains the lower parts of several medieval buildings including a hall block measuring 23m by 6m internally with a private room at the far end. A causeway ramp leads past where there was a guardhouse and through a range near the east end.

FAHY or DOONA   F754125

The NW corner of a tower 12m by 8.5m over walls 1.8m thick stands four storeys high with evidence of a passage and vault high up. The entrance probably faced east with the stair in the SE corner. Just 1m to the SE is a later house measuring 12m by 6m of two storeys and an attic.

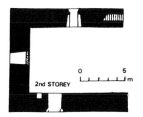

Plans of Doocastle

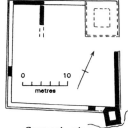

Creevagh: plan

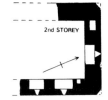

Plans of Killernan Castle

Gweeshadan Castle

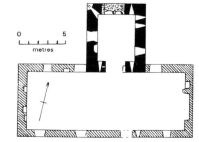

Plan of Island Castle

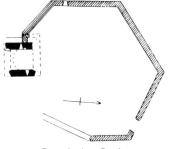

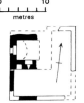

Gweeshadan Castle   *Kilquire: plan*   *Friarstown: plan*   *Inishmaine: plan*

FRIARSTOWN   G206126   D

This ivy-covered tower measuring 8m square has three storeys under a vault. A damaged entrance faces SE but there is no sign of a staircase or any mural rooms except a latrine in the west corner at second storey level and the unusual feature of a tiny circular room with gunloops in a single storey casemate on the north corner. This retains its roof of overlapping slabs although very little remains of the outer wall to support it.

GWEESHADAN   M210824   D

Parts of the sidewalls remain of a tower 7m wide with a narrow arch remaining of the vault between them. A turret, probably to contain a latrine, was later added to the north end of the west wall, which also has an added battered base. Abutting against the turret is the fragmentary 1.2m thick wall of a seven-sided bawn 26m across.

INISHMAINE   M139617   A

Although perhaps designed as a gatehouse to a monastic enclosure this structure looks like the 4.4m wide end wall of tower 9.3m wide built in two stages. Two storeys remain with an entrance with a drawbar slot and a wide spiral staircase. A short but massive low section of the north wall is all that remains of the added main body of the tower.

ISLAND   M470821

Earthworks surround the buried base of a building about measuring 15m by 9m, possibly an early hall house. The T-planned two storey 17th century house of the Dillon family lower down to the east uses as its north wing a two storey block measuring 7.3m by 6.3m over walls 1.2m thick well provided with gunloops, including one piercing the NW corner. This is a relic of a castle here belonging to the MacJordan Duff MacCostello.

KILLALA   G137281

A housing estate lies on the site of a palace of the bishops of Killala demolished in the 1950s. It was a three storey L-shaped mansion with a tower-like block at one end. It was restored from a ruinous condition c1800 but the see was amalgamated with Tuam in 1834 and the Heathfields took it over.

KILLERNAN   M266601

The northern half of a tower 10m wide retains part of a vault over the third storey. All that remains of the fourth storey is a thin wall set on the vault haunch which formed the inner wall of a mural chamber on the east side. The third storey had a latrine in the NW corner.

KILQUIRE   M235652   D

A pile of debris covers the base of the east end of a tower about 8m wide but the SW corner stands high with part of the basement vault and a latrine-chute on the south side. The tower occupied the NW corner of a bawn measuring 13.5m from north to south by 12m wide with its 1m thick wall still partly 2m high on the south side but reduced to footings on the east.

Killernan Castle

Kilquire Castle

Island Castle

KINLOUGH   M259504 C

This building measuring 12.3m by 10.7m at ground level is thought to be a 13th century structure, the only original upper level having a projecting latrine at the west end. The fireplace in the SW corner dates from a remodelling probably by Sir John MacOliver Burke, the owner in 1574, which provided two further storeys, also with corner fireplaces. There are no vaults or stairs of chambers in the walls, which are quite thin above the massive battered base in which are gunloops and an entrance with a drawbar slot. The castle was mortgaged to the Blakes in 1629, and they leased it to John Darcy in 1668.

KINTURK   M124839

Immediately north of the 17th century south range set on a cliff over a stream, and at an awkward angle to it, lies the 11m long and 3.3m thick south wall of an earlier O'Malley tower house containing an entrance passage flanked by a guard room and a passage to a destroyed spiral stair in the SW corner. The bawn measuring about 75m from north to south by 65m wide forming the largest castle enclosure now remaining in County Mayo dates from after the castle was taken over by Tiobod na Long Burke in the 1600s. There are square flankers with gunloops on the NE and SE corners of the bawn and at the SW corner there is a lofty third flanker at the corner of a range about 20m long by 8m wide with fireplaces in the south end wall. The more massively built south range projects beyond the bawn. Outside the bawn wall east of it is a level terrace above a cliff edge as far as the SE flanker, which contained three storeys of rooms.

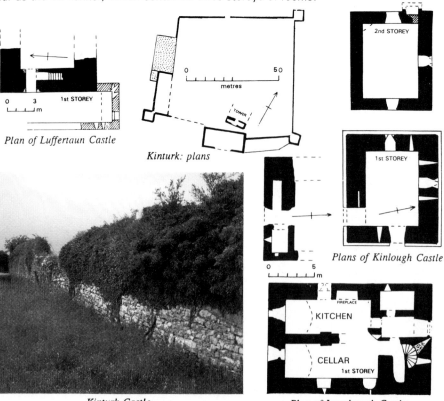

Plan of Luffertaun Castle

Kinturk: plans

2nd STOREY

1st STOREY

Plans of Kinlough Castle

Kinturk Castle

KITCHEN

CELLAR
1st STOREY

Plan of Loughmask Castle

Kinlough Castle

Loughmask Castle

LOUGHMASK   M143604

Maurice FitzGerald had a castle here which was captured by MacWilliam de Burgh in 1264 and which later passed to Sir William Liath de Burgh. The de Stauntons had custody here of Edmund, son of Richard de Burgh, "Red" Earl of Ulster, who was taken prisoner at the instigation of his namesake cousin. The castle was burnt by Brian O'Connor in 1412 during his conflict with Edmund Burke and is thought to have been rebuilt in the 1480s. It was captured in 1571 from John MacOliver Burke by a force led by the Earl of Clanricarde in conjunction with the English commanders Fitton and Malbie.

Amongst the outbuildings of a later mansion is a large four storey tower 18m long by 12m wide mostly or entirely dating from a rebuilding of 1618, that date and initials of Sir Thomas Burke and his wife Elles (Alice) Butler appearing on a fireplace. Sir Thomas, who died in 1642, last of the MacWilliam Iochtair Burkes, was the grandson of William Burke who had been granted Lough Mask in 1587. By 1669 the castle had passed to Tristan Beresford. The tower has side walls 1.6m thick and a lowest level divided by a longitudinal crosswall to carry two vaults, one of the rooms being a kitchen with a large fireplace. The thick east end wall contains a tier of chambers over the entrance and an unusually wide spiral staircase. There were attics within gables flush with the outer walls, although there were wall-walks along the north and south sides, square bartizans on the SE and NW corners, and a box-machicolation over the entrance.

LUFFERTAUN   M133794

A bawn wall with circular flankers on the east corners is represented by a ha-ha east of the 19th century house and outbuildings south and west of it. In the NW corner is the western part of a tower 10.6m wide with a rebuilt entrance and a straight staircase leading south. The gap between the entrance and a steep slope 4m away was later filled in by a building with gunloops opening out of the kitchen fireplace at the south end of it.

MACPHILBIN'S   M061816   D

Most of the 0.75m thick east wall survives of a bawn about 14m square perched on a hillock. There are remains of a gateway with a drawbar-slot and one gunloop facing south. Steps lead up to a narrow wall-walk of slabs projecting inwards, off which was access to a machicolation over the gateway. Very little remains of a circular flanker 4.5m in diameter at the NE corner and even less of a SW flanker of uncertain shape. In the NW corner is the lower part of a tower about 8.5m square, the NW corner of which still stands 4m high. Neither the entrance or a staircase remain. The castle belonged to the MacPhilbins

MANNIN   M452849

The lower parts remain of a circular keep 10.2m in diameter over walls 1.8m thick. Towards the SW and NW the tower has projecting semi-circular turrets, the latter having a latrine chute. Facing east is what appears to be the base of a porch for a lost upper entrance probably approached by a stair set upon the outer wall whose base lies along the SE part of the building. There is a blocked doorway opening towards the porch and there is a loop facing SE, both of them buried to a degree that suggests that the lowest storey floor can hardly have been higher than the surrounding bogland, originally a lake.

MOCORHA   M235538

Much of the remains of this building 9.6m wide possibly of 13th or 14th century origin are buried in rubble. A fragment of a vault remains, apparently an insertion upon an internal thickening of the walls which has blocked an original loop on the west side.

Mannin: plan

0   5
L_I_I_I_I_I m

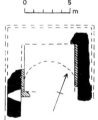

Mocorha: plan

0   10
L_I_I_I_I_I
metres

MacPhilbin's Castle

MacPhilbin's plan

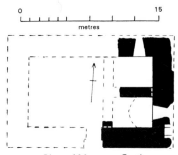

Plan of Murneen Castle

Murneen Castle

MOYNE   M256493   D

Adjoining a later ruined house is a fine round-cornered tower measuring 14.5m by 10.2m over walls 2.4m thick. It was probably built by one of the McWilliam Burkes in the late 15th century, later passing to the Barretts. The 3m thick east wall contains chambers reached off the spiral stair in the NE corner and the entrance lies on the north side adjacent to this staircase. The second storey has a fireplace in the north wall of the main room and a latrine in the SE corner. The rooms over the vault are no longer accessible.

MURNEEN   M353806   D

The lower parts of the east end of a 13th century hall house 12m wide over walls 2.2m thick and about 18m long survive on a ditched platform. The remaining end has a crosswall dividing into two cellars, one of which retains its vault. One jamb of an original ground floor entrance remains on the south side. Its position suggests that as modified in later years the building had a central cellar or corridor with pairs of vaulted cellars at each end. The latrine chute in the SE corner suggests that the upper storey had a private chamber at that end divided off from a hall in the western part.

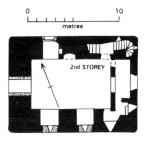

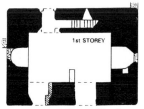

Plans of Moyne Castle

Mannin Castle

RAPPA   G184220   D

Occupied until about a hundred years ago, this ruin shows evidence of at least four phases of construction beginning probably in the 16th century with a MacWilliam Burke tower measuring 8.8m by 7.7m, later much altered but retaining corbels for a square bartizan upon the SE corner and the drawbar-slot of its north-facing entrance. In the 17th century a new three storey wing with fireplaces in end walls surmounted by diagonally-set chimney stacks was added in front of the entrance to make an L-plan building, but before long the re-entrant angle was filled in by another wing. The whole building was remodelled in the 19th century when a further wing was added on the east side.

RATHROE   G137281   D

The stair rising from the east-facing entrance of this Barrett tower measuring 10m by 9m only goes up to the second storey, where it ends in a passage to a latrine in the SW corner. The third storey loft and the mostly destroyed fourth storey above must have been reached by ladders. There are traces of a small square bawn to the east and north, the other sides being protected by the river.

ROCKFLEET or CARRIGAHOWLEY   L931953   B

At high tide the sea washes the foot of the east wall of this O'Malley tower to which, after the death of her second husband Sir Richard Burke in 1583, the celebrated pirate Grace O'Malley retired with "all of her followers and 1,000 head of cows and mares". Back in 1574 a English force sent out from Galway to capture it had been successfully driven off. The tower measures 9.6 by 8m at the base (which has modern patching on the east side) but rather less higher up because of the batter of the walls. There are four storeys with a vault over a dark loft at the third level, and gables on the east and west walls. The east wall contains narrow chambers, with an awkward ladder between the lowest two giving access to where a spiral stair begins in the SE corner. A tiny latrine opens off the stair. The topmost room has a fireplace on the south side and a doorway for hoisting up supplies set just east of the north-facing entrance (both openings have been renewed). The wall-walk has square bartizans set upon the SE and NW corners.

Rappa Castle

Shrule Castle

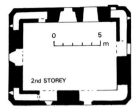

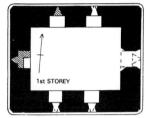

Plans of Shrule Castle

Rockfleet Castle

Turin Castle

Plans of Rockfleet Castle

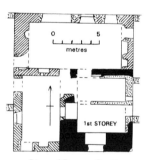

Plan of Rappa Castle

Rathroe: plans

SHRULE   M281591   A

Commanding the bridge is a 16th century tower which belonged to the chief of the MacWilliam Burke Iochtair family, who came to its relief in 1570 during an attack by the Lord President of Connacht and the Earl of Clanricarde. At each of the three unvaulted storeys the tower measures 9.9m by 6.8m inside. The walls are 2.6m thick at the base, where they incorporate part of a 13th century hall-house, but are battered so that at the third storey they are only 1.5m thick. This level has rooms in the western corners, a latrine chute in the NE corner, one mullion-and-transom window, and a straight flight of steps leading up around the SE corner. The corners are splayed off above the base and have bartizans with splayed off outer corners at the summit, where there was an attic room within the wall-walk.

TERMONCARRAGH   F655355

A wall 0.8m thick surrounds a bawn 32m by 26m. Just the west gable and south wall with gunloops remain of a house in the SW corner. Another Burke castle lay to the east at 750400.

Rappa Castle

TURIN   M275576   C

There was a castle here in the late 14th century but the existing tower measuring 11m by 8.2m is rather later and was held by Walter MacReamond Burke in 1574. There is a tier of chambers over the entrance in the east wall and a spiral stair in the NE corner. A loop from the basement covers the entrance since its doorway off the lobby further north than the outer doorway. The third storey has a fireplace on the west and a latrine on the north, plus a chamber with an angle loop in the NW corner. The fourth storey also has a fireplace and is vaulted, there being a passage along the north wall at that height. Most of the large and thinner walled single room on the fifth storey and the parapet with a machicolation over the entrance date from a restoration begun in 1997 and recently completed. See p85.

OTHER CASTLE REMAINS IN COUNTY MAYO

ACHILLBEG M707926 Footings of gatehouse in isolating ditch of promontory fort.
AHENA M284739 Buried base of tower 9m square on side of platform 30m by 24.
BALLYBACKAGH M246542 The lower part of a tower remains amongst farm buildings. The only feature not obscured by debris or vegetation is a latrine-chute facing west.
BALLYNACASHLAN G115409 Lower parts of side-walls 2.2m thick (one now part of field boundary) of tower 8.8m wide and probably at least 12m long.
BARRANAGH or BINGHAM's F652265 Two fragmentary walls 0.9m thick at high water line of Elly Harbour. A Barrett castle, later held by the Binghams.
BELLABURKE M099814 Base of NW and SW walls of tower about 12m by 10m with latrine chute in north corner. Traces of NW wall of bawn to SW.
BROCKAGH M016907 Ivy-clad lump 4m high of SW corner on ledge above river.
BUNARROWER L795796 One fallen fragment upon debris mound with abandoned later buildings. The castle belonged to the O'Malleys.
CAHERDOONGUNN M167608 Only footings remain of the wall of a bawn.
CARROWKEEL M223961 Possible footings of tower house.
CLOONKEEGHAN M249645 Pile of debris against north wall partly still 3m high.
CARROWNLOUGH M401678 Ringfort on hillock with traces of walling on south side. Possibly a 13th century castle. No remains of later castle to SE at M404676.
CASTLE HAG M147659 Partly mortared wall 5m high around court 32m across on island in Lough Mask. Possibly Irish-built, but destroyed by Felim O'Connor in 1233.
CASTLE ISLAND M187723 Remains of building 12m by 7m on island in Lough Carra.
CASTLE ISLAND G155142 Slight remains of O'Connor castle on island in Lough Conn.
CASTLENAGEELHA G209348 Ramp behind turret at south end leads to top of drystone rampart 2.5m thick cutting off west side of headland 28m by 18m.
CASTLEREAGH G172313 Lower part of north wall and other footings of bawn about 17m by 32m probably with central tower. Probably the O'Kelly castle of Doonamona.
CASTLETOWN M175609 Very ruinous lower part of tower 10.2m by 8.4m with shed replacing SE corner. Latrine-chute on north side. See plan.

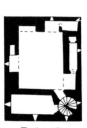
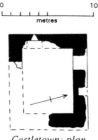
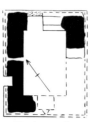
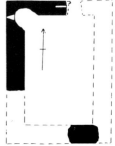

Turin: plan   *Castletown: plan*   *Cloghans: plan*   *Crossmolina: plan*

CLOGHAN LUCAS M214802 Featureless lower parts of supposed 13th century hall-house 9.6m by 7.8m lying within ditched enclosure. See plan below.
CLOGHANS M313633 Lower parts of tower 11.2m by 9.2 over walls 2.2m thick. NE wall has entrance and stair. Latrine-chute in displaced part of NW wall. See plan p86.
CLOUNGEE G263008 Traces of 1.3m thick west and north walls of tower 13.7m by 11m amid debris.
CROSSMOLINA G136177 Fragmentary building 15m long and 11 or 12m wide on a hillock. Drawbar-slot of entrance on north and stairwell in NW corner. Plan p86.
DOONAMOE F645375 Promontory with drystone wall at neck and traces of gatehouse.
DOONCASTLE 042840 Fragment of NW corner 2m high and low fragment of NE corner of a MacPhilbin tower 13.5m long on a crescent-shaped platform upon a hillock.
DUNDONNELL F778274 Platform 25m by 10m on coastal promontory with traces of guardhouse 7.5m by 4.8m over walls up to 1.6m thick.
ELLISTRON M240610 2m thick north wall with long passage at level of the vaulted second storey to latrine from stairwell in the NE corner.
HOLLYMOUNT M263687 Possible remains of tower in later house.
KILKEERAN M227568 Later ruined house close to north side of lower part of tower 8m wide with interior buried by debris.
KNOCKCAUNAKILL M293792 Low shapeless fragment and part of footings of tower.
KNOCKMARIA G152096 Low shapeless fragment remains of the NE corner of a tower.
KNOCKROE M306605 Fallen fragment 1.4m thick containing latrine shaft.
LISKILLEEN M205679 Very fragmentary and partly drystone wall around bawn 70m by 60m containing buried base of former MacDonnell tower to NE of centre.
MOYHENNA M220918 Just one small fallen fragment remains of a Burke tower.
PORTNAHOLLY G115409 NE and SW walls 1.5m high with latrine-chute of tower 15m by 7m on rock by harbour.
ROBEEN M233690 Fragment of west wall 2m thick above wide battered base and NW corner of substantial building.
Debris pile only: BALLYMARTIN M237603, CUILBAUN G261009, TOGHER M234728
Earthworks only: CLOONKELLY G150150, CLOONTALLY G179164, INISHCOE G150150, RATH M461882, TERRYBAUN G190056
The structure on Illanacurra Island, Lough Carra M196717 is probably drystone cashel.

SITES OF CASTLES IN COUNTY MAYO

0 _____ 25

BALLYSAKEERY G245271 Barrett castle later held by Burkes.
CARRICKCANASS G158332 Possibly a de Burgh foundation, later held by MacPaddins. Site beside stream.
CASTLELACKAN G176367 House on site of MacEgan Castle.
CORTHANAN G140116 Castle destroyed by O'Donnells in 1526 lay west of 1838 house.
CUSLOUGH M152649 Site of 13th century hall house.

Plan of Castle Hag

FARRAGH G184277 Site of "castle and bawne".
RINNAHULTY M224884 House on site of castle may incorporate old parts.
WESTPORT M989845 O'Malley castle replaced by 17th century house, itself replaced by Colonel John Browne's house of 1730.
OTHER CASTLE SITES: Ballyduffy G126111, Ballynaslee M159729, Belclare L958824, Belleck-Moy G253197, Callinteenaun G205264, Carraholly L956854, Castlehill F800067, Castletown M185520, Castlekeel M358716, Castlekirke G269043, Cong M147553, Coolcon M329645, Corlogh F664356, Danganmore M249929, Enagh More M117182, Inver F781352, Kilgalligan F793410, Kilkeeran M227548, Kilquire M256617, Knockalina F764356, Knockalegan M282700, Knockglass G515202, Meelick G209289, Rubble G354032, Shanclogh G237112, Termon F616203, Tiraun F621238, Tulrohaun M453730, Turlough M205935, Woodstock M382710

GAZETTEER OF CASTLES IN COUNTY ROSCOMMON

BALLINTOBER   M726748   A

This spacious courtyard castle of c1300 measures 80m by 73m inside a wall 1.7m thick
fronted by a moat still full of water on the west. The gatehouse 13.4m wide on the east
side with twin polygonal-fronted towers is now very fragmentary but much of the curtain
stands complete with several inserted gunloops, a staircase on the north side and four
polygonal corner towers averaging 8.4m wide. The western towers stand highest and are
said to have been occupied until the 19th century. The NW tower contains a fireplace
dated 1627 and was rebuilt at that time with a new thick end wall containing a spiral
staircase and a tier of chambers over an entrance protected by a machicolation. The inner
part of the SW tower, with a turret with latrines on the east and traces of a spiral stair on
the south is thought to be original work of c1300. These towers contained chambers
serving a hall or pair of halls set by the curtain between them. The NE tower projected
more boldly than the other three and was basically a square with a polygonal north end.

The castle was probably built by Richard de Burgh, although Leask claimed it was built
by the O'Connors, a junior branch of whom captured the castle in 1315. Then known as
Toberbride, it was back in de Burgh hands in 1333. From 1385 until 1657 Ballinitober was
the seat of the chiefs known as O'Connor Don. The castle suffered several sieges during
the 15th century and in 1579 Hugh O'Connor Don was forced to ally himself with Red
Hugh O'Donnell against the English after O'Donnell breached the walls of Ballintober with
the aid of Spanish cannon. The castle was a centre of Catholic resistance in the wars of
the 1640s and held out against Lord Ranelagh and Sir Charles Coote in 1642. Although
confiscated by Cromwell it was recovered by O'Connor Don in 1677.

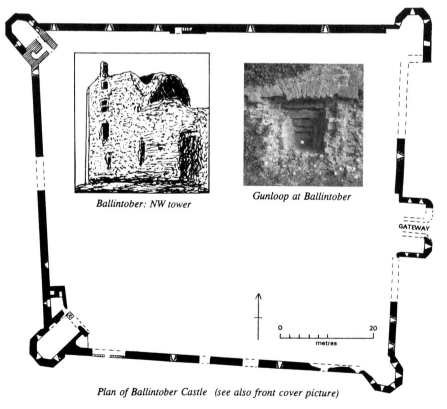

Ballintober: NW tower

Gunloop at Ballintober

GATEWAY

0   20
metres

Plan of Ballintober Castle (see also front cover picture)

Ballyleague Castle

Canbo Castle

BALLYLEAGUE N004695 C

There are no remains of the castle recorded here in 1220 and 1227, which was probably a motte, but a late medieval tower house measuring 12m by 8.2m still has three levels of rooms, all with fireplaces in the east wall, under a top vault. The second storey has finely made round-headed loops with a bottom slot for handguns. There may have been stairs in the very damaged projection at the SE corner.

CANBO M888951 C

The east end remains of a stronghouse 7.8m wide over walls 1.1m thick, and it is said to have been 16m long. The only features are the south-facing doorway with a drawbar slot, and a second storey loop and third storey fireplace in the east end wall. It is probably early 17th century, but a castle here is recorded in 1536, and a bawn was recorded in 1650.

CASTLE MORE M605943

Footings and fallen fragments 2m thick remain of the north and west walls of a tower 14m by 11m lying within a platform with evidence of a former bawn wall and an outbuilding. The castle was captured by Turlough O'Connor in 1336 and in 1595 was surrendered to the MacDiarmatas, allies of O'Donnell.

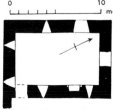

Ballyleague: plan

Loop at Ballyleague

Canbo: plan

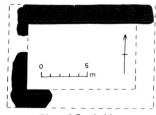

Plan of Castle More

Coote Hall

Cloonbigny Castle

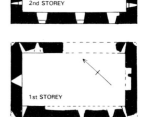

Plan of Cloonbigny Castle

Plan of Cloghan Castle

Plans of Dundonnell Castle

CLOGHAN   M844508

There is a sheila-na-gig on the 12m high southern corner of this O'Donnellan tower measuring 12m by 10m over walls 2m thick. The SE side is thicker to contain mural chambers, the lowest of which, opening off the entrance passage, has a gunloop with two oillets side-by-side. Single oillets open off the staircase in the south corner.

CLOONBIGNY   M875384   D

What little remains of the lower parts of the main body of a tower house about 12m long by 8.5m wide perched on a glacial mound is buried in debris, but parts of the SE end wall stand two storeys high with slight remains of the stairwell in the south corner. Abutting against this part, which was built before the main body, is the SW end wall of a 17th century house 16.4m long by 7.6m wide of two storeys and an attic with fireplaces in projecting breasts in the end walls. The house has large windows facing SE. It has lost much of its NW wall, although a doorway jamb remains there with a drawbar slot.

COOTEHALL   G894038   D

Sir Charles Coote's 55m square bawn of c1620 remains fairly intact except for the SW corner flanker and parts of the adjoining walls. The other flankers are circular 5.5m in diameter with gunloops and fireplaces backing against where a prow eliminates any dead ground on the outermost part of the circle. On the south side an inhabited house extends from the SE flanker to where there is a fragment of the internal house.

Dundonnell Castle

Dunamon Castle

DRUMDOE G807096

One corner of a MacDermot Roe tower measuring about 12m by 8m stands three storeys high with gunloops, windows and a basement fireplace. To the north and NE is a bawn with a wall 3m high with six gunloops, a gatehouse, and a flanker at the north corner.

DUNAMON M799648

Now adapted as a religious establishment, with a 19th century extension at one end and a corridor at the other end linking it to a 1960s block, this is an H-shaped building measuring 24.3m by 15.3m overall, but with recesses 4m wide and 2.7m deep in the centre of each long side of the lowest two storeys. Arches carry the third storey over the recesses and all three levels have many mullion-and-transom windows, whilst at the top the roof has three gables on each of the long sides. This structure must date from a rebuilding of 1620, but there seems to have been a fortress here as early as 1154, and the de Stauntons and their successors the de Birminghams had a castle here which was destroyed by the O'Connors in 1233, 1315 and 1400, but rebuilt by the MacDavid Burkes. It was granted in 1652 to Robert King, whose son John was later made Lord Kingston, but the Caulfields leased the lands and retained an interest in the property until 1920.

DUNDONNELL M894380

Lying within a ringfort forming a bawn 50m by 44m is a stronghouse 14m long by 8m wide over walls 1.2m thick. There are gunloops near the corners of the lower storey, which is much defaced internally, whilst the upper storey has fireplaces with lofty chimney stacks at each end and three large windows in the one side-wall remaining complete.

GALEY M956587 G

A ditch isolates a platform beside Loch Ree in which lies a four storey fragment of a tower 11m wide with traces of a vault which may have been inserted, since it appears to partly obscure a window embrasure on the second storey, adjacent to which is a latrine.

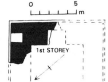

Galey: plan

MOYVANNAN M979479

This four storey tower measures 8.3m by 7.3m and is dated 1501 on one of the quoins. Originally a rectory, a church was later added to the NNW of it, and both parts now form a residence, having been remodelled and castellated in the 19th century.

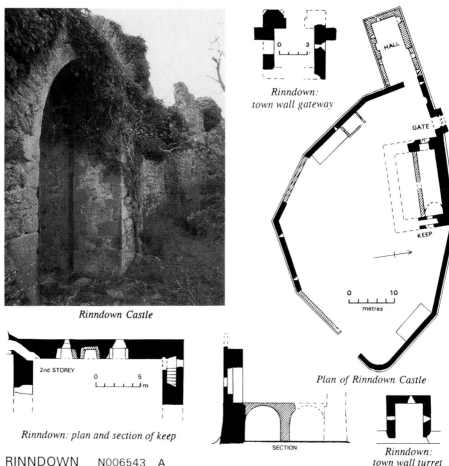

Rinndown:
town wall gateway

Rinndown Castle

HALL

GATE

KEEP

0 ——— 10
metres

2nd STOREY

0 ——— 5
m

Plan of Rinndown Castle

Rinndown: plan and section of keep

SECTION

Rinndown:
town wall turret

RINNDOWN   N006543   A

Geoffrey de Marisco erected a ringwork on a promontory on the west side of Lough Ree in 1227. It was stormed and burnt by Felim O'Connor in 1236 and the stone curtain around an elliptical court 38m by 58m and the keep on the north side were erected by Henry III between then and 1260. The keep measured 19m by 13.5m over walls 2.6m thick and has a longitudinal crosswall to carry inserted vaults below the hall itself, which retains a fireplace. The south side has vanished but the north wall forming part of the bailey enceinte still stands complete to the wall-walk 10m above ground. The east wall contains a service stair down to the cellars and probably had the hall entrance at its southern end. Immediately west of the keep is a gatehouse 5.2m by 3.5m with a groove for a portcullis. Further large sums were spent on the castle by Edward I in 1273-9, and in 1299-1302 Robert de Oxford was in charge of the construction of a new hall at a cost of £113. This must be the two storey structure projecting entirely beyond the west end of the bailey. Both this building and the curtain wall show signs of considerable 16th century rebuilding with gunloops in the newer parts. A town lay north of the castle with a thin 500m long wall cutting off the promontory neck to protect it. Long stretches still survive along with parts of a 7m square central gatehouse and a turret 4.8m wide projecting 3.8m, although the settlement it enclosed was mostly abandoned by c1400.

ROSCOMMON   M872651   A

The castle fortified by the Justiciar, Robert de Ufford in 1269 at a cost of £98 was soon wrecked by Aedh O'Connor, although the rectangular secondary gatehouse 11.4m by 8.8m on the west site may be a relic of it. During the ten years following Aedh's death in 1274 the castle was rebuilt, the Irish Pipe Rolls recording £3,200 being spent upon it in 1277-8. The result was a court 52m by 40m enclosed by walls 2.5m thick flanked by three-storey U-shaped corner towers 10.5m in diameter with straight staircases. On the east is a huge gatehouse 22.2m wide with a long passage flanked by round-fronted towers. No stairs survive but the northern tower has a latrine at ground level.

Donogh O'Kelly captured the castle in 1308. The O'Connors held it from 1340 until it was captured in 1569 by Sir Henry Sidney, although they briefly lost it in 1499, when it

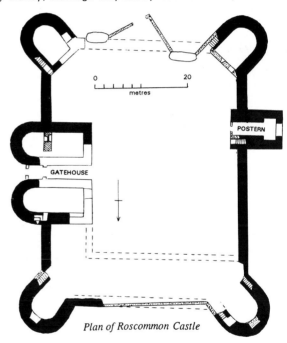

was captured by the Earl of Kildare, and in 1544, when it was granted to MacWilliam Burke. In the 1580s the castle was remodelled as the chief residence of Sir Nicholas Malby, Governor of Connacht, a fine new range being built on the north side, where the corner towers were given new floor levels and many mullion-and-transom windows in the upper two levels. Windows of this type also survive in the gatehouse. The Confederate Catholics captured the castle in 1645. All the internal walls have been destroyed and the north and south curtains were blown up by the Cromwellian commander Reynalds after the castle was surrendered to him in 1652. Probably also destroyed about that time was a thin outer wall fronting a moat, and the walls and circular corner bastions laid out around the town to the south during the 1570s. See page 1.

Plan of Roscommon Castle

Roscommon Castle

OTHER CASTLES IN COUNTY ROSCOMMON

ATHENLEAGUE M829578 Three storey 6.4m square wings on east side and north and south gables with fireplaces remain of main block 16.4m by 7.6m, also of three storeys. The building has thin walls without any defensive features.

BALLAGH M930529 Only a pile of debris remains of an O'Kelly castle.

BALLANGARE M751877 18th century house in NW corner of bawn 34m square now missing its south wall and SE corner. O'Connor tower house site to west.

BOYLE G805028 Cloister of Cistercian abbey converted into bawn with east range adapted as house and rectangular two storey gatehouse added on west side. See p10.

CALLOW M711958 1.5m high west wall 0.6m thick of bawn 77m by 60m. Drystone wall on east and ditch on west and south sides.

CASTLE NAUGHTON M960447 Footings of building 16m by 10m on 10m high motte.

CASTLE SAMPSON M933416 South wall 5m high and 1.8m thick of possible hall-house about 17m long with join between it and SE turret 5.3m by 3m. Footings of north wall.

CLOONGLASNY M973893 Only a D-shaped enclosure with a bank and ditch remains, the tower in the NE corner having vanished.

CORREEN M915264 Two storey inhabited stronghouse with porch in middle of east side and stair turret in middle of west side. Castellated and much altered in 19th century.

KILLEGLAN M882407 Fragment of east gable and footings of other walls of building.

LIBERTY M954338 Fragment of NE corner of castle later held by Theobald, Lord Dillon.

LONGFIELD M897521 Edward Coyle's T-plan stronghouse of 1646 has a wing 4.4m by 3m on one side of a main block 11m by 7.6m over walls 1.2m thick. Rebuilt in 1675 but abandoned by 1824.

LOUGH GLINN M628867 Ivy-covered three storey high corner tower of Desmond castle

MILLTOWN M875449 Slight traces of former building on a mound.

MOYLURG M842989 Tower 14.3m by 9m over walls 1.6m thick with fragments of bawn to south with evidence of two storey circular SW flanker.

TOBERAVADY M814590 Fragments of bawn with south corner flanker and fireplace nearby, plus NE end wall of range with evidence of two storeys and an attic in the roof.

TULSK M8080 Buried footings of circular tower on low motte with two baileys. The castle belonged to O'Connor Roe in the 15th century. See page 5.

TULLY M941304 Recently destroyed stronghouse 17.6m by 9m with chimney stacks on end gables and 4m diameter flankers with gunloops on western corners. Originally had a bawn to the east with other flankers. See page 10.

Thinly-walled 17th century houses without defensive features:
Corkip M930425, Elphin Bishop's Palace M873889, Kellybrook M952552 (still inhabited), Lough Scur N034084.

Mocmoyne M800029 has a 17th century earthwork fort.

Ringworks: Ballyglass M754848, Creeharmore M816489, Gortnasillagh M773814, Rathmore M831870, Rathnalong M788849. Mottes: Mullagh M960448, Oran 7060

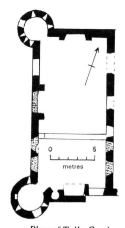

SITES OF CASTLES IN ROSCOMMON

Ballinlough M582775, Ballyhahough M840980, Bunnamucka M917815, Carrowphadeen M995496, Castle Island M847045, Castle Leland M833810, Castle Plunket M776786, Castle Ruby M789803, Castletown M851940, Clonark M982356, Cloonburren M982288, M851940, Coolnageer M923496, Cortober M937992, Crunaun M599924, Cuilleen M905333, Curraghboy M934470, Curryroe M980385, Dangan M979937, Demesne M679801, Fairymount M934719, Kellybrooke M953556, Knockroe M877945, Leitrim M886739, Lisdaulin M919569, Roxborough M897679, Scregg M930557, Tonvy M934308

Plan of Tully Castle

ARDNABRONE   G539343

A 16m long and 1.1m thick fragment with a wall-walk and a projecting second storey latrine remains of the south side of a bawn of the O'Dowds of Tireragh. A second fragment with a corner bartizan lies 31m to the NE, with buried footings between them

ARDTERMON   G588434   C

Sir Nathaniel Gore's early 17th century stronghouse was restored as a residence a few years ago. Of three storeys with an attic in the roof, it measures 35m by 8m and has circular flankers 5.2m in diameter furnished with gunloops on the eastern corners. On the west side a larger semi-circular tower containing a doorway and staircase around a central well faces towards a bawn with a south range and a NW flanker. The bawn gateway on the north side has a drawbar slot. The house also has an east doorway with a gunloop in the jamb and fireplaces on the west and at either end. See page 3.

BALLINAFAD   G781087   B

Captain St John Barbe built this castle c1590-1610 and installed a garrison of ten men under a constable. In 1641 it resisted the Confederate Irish until the garrison ran out of water. The three storey main block 10.6m by 8m with a fireplace at one end of the basement is dwarfed by four 6m diameter corner towers with high chimneys and machicolations. One tower contained a wooden staircase with a second storey entrance beside it. The other towers contained tiers of rectangular private rooms.

0   10
metres

Ardtermon Castle

Plan of Ardnabrone Castle

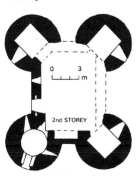

0   3
m

2nd STOREY

Plan of Ballinafad Castle

Ballinafad Castle

Bawnmoyle Castle

Ballincar Castle

BALLINCAR   G667391

This three storey T-plan house belonged to the O'Harts but later passed to the Griffiths family. It has a three bay long main block measuring 16.2m by 7.7m with fireplaces and chimney stacks in the end gables. The only defensive features of the thinly walled building are the loops on ether side of the 7.2m wide wing projecting 8.8m from the middle of the west side. The central part of the main block probably formed a staircase hall.

BALLINDOON   G792134   D

The lower parts of the north and west walls of a probable 13th century hall-keep 15m long by 11m wide lie near the east side of Lough Arrow. It lies in the SE corner of an enclosure with footings of a wall in the rampart around the NE corner and a higher fragment facing a ditch extending to the lough on the north. In the later medieval period this was an important seat of the MacDonagh family, who founded the nearby friary.

Ballymote Castle

BALLYMOTE   G661155   B

Richard de Burgh's castle of c1290-1300 has 2.8m thick curtain walls surviving intact around a court about 38m square. There are round towers about 9m in diameter at all four corners and there are D-shaped towers on the east and west sides, but only the stub remains of a square back gateway on the south side and only footings of the outer parts of a gatehouse 23m wide on the north side with a passageway between two U-shaped towers. It seems that an intended rock-cut moat was never completed although the land outside the walls probably had a shallow covering of water anyway.

In the early 14th century the castle fell to the O'Connors. Although claimed by O'Connor Sligo as his, and surrendered by him to the English authorities in 1571, the castle was mostly held by the MacDonaghs between the 1380s and the 1560s. Richard Bingham captured the castle in 1584 and the O'Connors burnt it in 1588. It was recaptured by the MacDonaghs in 1598 and sold to the O'Donnells, who surrendered it to the English in 1602. About this time the SE tower was rebuilt as a tower house with a straight thick wall towards the court containing an entrance and stair. The Taaffes held Ballymote from at least the 1630s until 1652. Lord Granard captured the castle from Captain Terence MacDonagh in 1690 and the outer part of the gatehouse then destroyed.

BAWNMOYLE   G566346

Projecting from the east side of the drystone rampart of a ringfort about 40m across used as a bawn is the lowest storey of a tower measuring 9.5m by 8.3m over walls 2m thick. The west wall has remains of a staircase rising from an entrance flanked by a chamber so low it can probably have only been suitable for a guard-dog. Each of the other walls has an embrasure with a loop, that on the north also having a gunloop flanking the rampart.

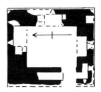

Bawnmoyle: plan

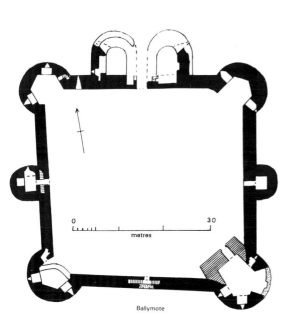

Ballymote

Plan of Ballymote Castle

0   5
metres

2nd STOREY

1st STOREY

Plans of Ballincar Castle

Castle Baldwin

Cottlestown Castle

Plan of Cottlestown Castle

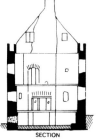

Plan & section of Castle Baldwin

CASTLETOWN   G378286   D

On the west side of the Easky River are remains of a MacDonnell castle just 200m away from their tower of Roslee. Low fragments remain of the side-walls of a building 9.6m wide over walls 2m thick and probably at least 15m long, possibly a hall-house. It evidently remained in use until the 17th century since there are remains at its south end of a small court with several gunloops facing east towards the river. See pages 9 & 101.

CASTLE BALDWIN   G757144   A

The projecting wing of this thinly walled early 17th century stronghouse measuring 12.7m by 8.7m is thought to have contained a wooden staircase. There were two storeys of living rooms over a very low service basement partly below ground level with a fireplace at one end, plus an attic within a narrow wall-walk and parapet with a machicolation over the entrance.

COTTLESTOWN   G290260

Donnell O'Dowd is said to have built a castle here in the 1440s but the existing three storey stronghouse 18m long by 9m wide over walls 1.6m thick at the battered base probably dates from the early 17th century. It has been much altered over the years and a water tank has been built upon one of the two square bartizans at the SE and NW corners. Indications of a late date are the lack of any stone staircase and the presence of a wide kitchen fireplace, now blocked, at ground level in the west end wall. The basement loops (only one looks authentic) appear to have been reset into blocked up wider openings. After the O'Dowds were dispossessed by Cromwell in 1653 the castle was granted to Robert Morgan and either he or his son built a new house nearby to the SE.

Drumcondra: plan

Grangemore: plans

2nd STOREY

1st STOREY

Grangemore Castle

Plan of Dargan Castle

Drumcondra Castle

DARGAN   G724280

One fragment of a tower measuring about 15m by 11m over walls 2.1m thick with a corner and a straight staircase stands high on a rock above the lough. About 28m away is another fragment with a stub of walling 1.5m thick adjoining a more thinly walled structure which contained a small vaulted room, possibly part of a small twin-towered gatehouse. The castle was built in the 1420s by the MacDonough lord of Tirerrill and was captured in 1516 by the O'Donnells as part of an internal MacDonough family feud.

DRUMCONDRA   G745277   D

A hillock surrounded by marshes bears a bawn 24m by 19m enclosed by a wall 1m thick, now very fragmentary and in places patched with drystone walling. Gunloops lie either side of the east facing entrance. The SW corner contains the northern half of a thinly walled tower about 8m square now standing two storeys high with traces of a former stair in the NW corner beside the entrance.

GRANGEMORE   G457323   C

Just 5.3m due west of the ruined church is a tower measuring 8.2m by 7.8m containing an upper room presumably for a priest with a latrine in the SW corner over a lofty vaulted basement. The tower entrance and a doorway in the church SW corner almost face each other and were probably connected by a timber passageway. Above the entrance is a secret room reached by a trapdoor from a mural room in the SE corner.

INISHCRONE   G292302   D

The east end wall and two of the four circular corner turrets 4.6m in diameter with numerous gunloops of this early 17th century stronghouse have vanished. The main block measured about 14m by 8m and contained just one storey of living rooms over a basement with a kitchen fireplace at the west end, and an entrance with a drawbar slot on the north. Above was an attic containing servants' rooms.

MOYGARA   G688026   C

Only the featureless lowest level with its interior filled with rubble now remains of a building measuring 19m by 13m which may have been a 13th century hall-house built by the Cuisins family. The O'Garas took it over as their chief seat by 1338 and in the early 17th century they erected a bawn about 70m square with the older building lying in the middle of its north side. The bawn has a loopholed wall 1.1m thick with a tower 7m square at each corner. Three of them are of two storeys but the SW tower formed a tower house of three unvaulted storeys with the upper levels linked by a timber stair in a recess in the south wall. The bawn has a two storey gatehouse on the west side with remains of machicolations on the outer face, and there is a secondary entrance facing east, both archways retaining drawbar slots. See print on page 3.

MOYMLOUGH   G631250   C

On a platform partly enclosed by a ditch is a four storey O'Hara tower measuring 13.8m by 9.9m over walls 2.2m thick. A straight stair starts some way above ground in the broken end of the south wall and it is likely that the missing SE corner contained the entrance doorway. A 1.6m thick stub of a possible bawn wall adjoins the north end wall.

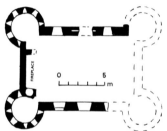

Plan of Inishcrone Castle

Moymlough Castle

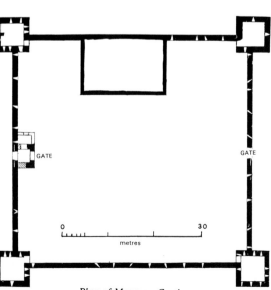

Plan of Moygara Castle

Inishcrone Castle

ROSLEE   G375385

Roslee belonged to the MacDonnells, originally gallowglass or mercenaries serving under the O'Dowds. By the shore is a tower 11.9m by 8.8m over walls about 2m thick perhaps of 14th century date since the blocked entrance doorway facing east has a voissoired head. From it rises a straight stair to the room over the vault, which has a latrine in the NW corner, and then a second straight stair in the south wall rose to the third storey and wall-walk. There are turrets on the northern corners but no bartizans, nor any fireplaces. A print and plan of 1792 show part of a bawn to the east and south with a pointed-arched entrance in a two storey north range adjoining the tower.

Rosslee Castle

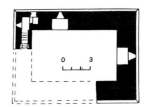

Moymlough: plan

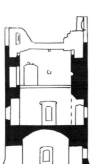

Castletown: plan

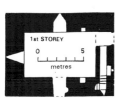

Plans and section of Roslee Castle

Moygara Castle

TANREGO   G600314

Originally built by the MacSwineys, this now very overgrown bawn was held by the Irvines from the 1650s until the 1850s. A wall with loopholes on the south and east encloses an irregularly shaped area 34m by 24m with a later house on the east against a thicker and probably older length of walling. The entrance lies at the north end of the west wall and there are semi-circular flankers in the middle of the south side and almost at the east end of the north side, which has a change of alignment halfway along its length.

TEMPLEHOUSE   G618182

Most of the west wall is missing of this hall keep measuring 21.2m by 11.2m over walls up to 2.4m thick which probably contained a hall and chamber end to end on the upper storey, the chamber having a latrine in a projection added to the south wall. Straight stairs rise to the wall-head from a north-facing upper window embrasure but no lower stairs remain. In a later medieval rebuilding, when the SW corner was replaced, the basement was later given two long parallel vaults supported on a central row of four piers but only one pier and one bay of vaulting now remain. Only the NE corner and the adjoining wall 1.8m thick remain of a bawn about 36m square to the east, but there is also an impressive fragment of the northern half of a gatehouse about 7m square with a murder-hole in the outer archway. A secondary gateway on the east side adjoins a thinly walled house replacing the original outer wall. It has remains of large three-light mullioned windows of c1600 on the second and third storeys, although the building was later drastically remodelled. It has fragments of two wings projecting to the west.

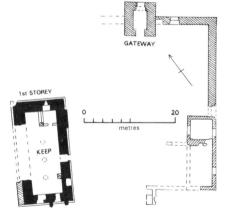

Plan of Templehouse Castle

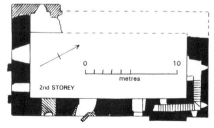

Templehouse Castle

Keep plan, Templehouse

OTHER CASTLE REMAINS IN COUNTY SLIGO

ANNAGHGOWLA G778138 Slight remains of castle on island in Lough Arrow.
BALLYNARAW G598118 Footings and one slightly higher fragment of east corner of tower measuring about 13.2m by 10.4m set beside a stream.
BEHY G719194 NW corner of MacDonagh tower 11.4m long over walls 2m thick. Traces of second storey vault. Sheila-na-gig in nearby shed. Held by Lord Dillon in 1624.
BELCLARE G386096 Ivy-clad three storey high north corner with traces of spiral staircase of O'Hara tower about 10m by 8m over walls 1.5m thick.
BRICKLIEVE G736141 Fragment of east wall of MacDonogh tower on platform. Occupied in 1593 by Gilbert Green.
CARRICK G759231 One loopholed wall 1.2m thick and 13.6m long, defaced on the inside, and fragments of two adjoining walls of small bawn.
CARROWLOUGHLIN G621109 Thin footings of large building or small open court.
CARTRONMORE G681440 Fragment 1.5m high and 0.9m thick of O'Connors' bawn which passed to the Parkes family in the 1650s and then to Gores.
CASTLE CARRAGH G435133 Tumbled fragments of O'Hara tower on overgrown crag.
CLOONMACDUFF G685269 Scanty traces of MacDonagh bawn with square flankers.
COOLBEG G667423 Low remains of tower 8m by 7m over walls 1.3m thick by shore.
DERRYMORE M714998 Slight remains of castle on island in Lough Gara.
DOONFORE G614458 A 20m long fragment of a bawn wall 2.5m high has a staircase built into it. It belonged to the Hart family. See photo on page 8.
GRANGE G636336 Fragmentary and defaced 20m long section of wall 1.1m thick rising 2m above bawn but 4m above ground to south. Contains an archway and two loops.
LACKAN G301331 Slight traces of tower of the MacCribhsighs, poets and historiographers to the O'Dowds of Tireragh from the 14th century until the 1650s.
RATHLEE G322374 Late 18th century signal tower on site of O'Dowd castle.
SLIGO G691361 Important 13th century courtyard castle, now vanished. Captured by O'Donnells in 1516 with assistance from guns of a French ship.
There is a 40m square star-fort at Bellaghy G479024, and there is an 18m square fort on Coney Island.

0 10 metres

Carrick: plan

SITES OF CASTLES IN COUNTY SLIGO

Bellanaboy G407234, Cabraghkeel G309359, Carrowcashel
   G744208, Carrowgobbadagh G674305, Dunneil G431336,
   Falduff G502117, Grange G659496, Hazelwood G727342, Kingsfort G765278,
   Knockmullin G671240, Lissadill G624441 & 619440, Tullanaclug G477115

INDEX OF STONE CASTLES IN CONNACHT